Ethics and the School Administrator

Balancing Today's Complex Issues

DAN MAHONEY

Rowman & Littlefield Education
Lanham, Maryland • Toronto • Plymouth, UK
2006

Published in the United States of America
by Rowman & Littlefield Education
A Division of Rowman & Littlefield Publishers, Inc.
A wholly owned subsidary of The Rowman & Littlefield Publishing Group, Inc.
4501 Forbes Boulevard, Suite 200, Lanham, Maryland 20706
www.rowmaneducation.com

Estover Road
Plymouth PL6 7PY
United Kingdom

British Library Cataloguing in Publication Information Available

Library of Congress Cataloging-in-Publication Data

Mahoney, Daniel J., 1953–
    Ethics and the school administrator : balancing today's complex issues / Dan
Mahoney.
        p.   cm.
    Includes bibliographical references and index.
    ISBN-13: 978-1-57886-493-5 (hardcover : alk. paper)
    ISBN-10: 1-57886-493-3 (hardcover : alk. paper)
    ISBN-13: 978-1-57886-494-2 (pbk. : alk. paper)
    ISBN-10: 1-57886-494-1 (pbk. : alk. paper)
    1. School administrators–Professional ethics–United States.   2. Deception–
United States.   3. Organizational sociology.   I. Title.
LB2831.82.M34   2006
174′.9371–dc22   2006014480

⊚ ™ The paper used in this publication meets the minimum requirements of
American National Standard for Information Sciences—Permanence of Paper for
Printed Library Materials, ANSI/NISO Z39.48-1992. Manufactured in the United
States of America.

For Mom and Dad—
Thank you for everything

Contents

Preface

Perhaps you are browsing through this book at a conference. Perhaps you are looking through it for the first time in one of your graduate courses. Whether you are a principal, program director, superintendent, member of a school board, or studying to be a school administrator, *Ethics and the School Administrator: Balancing Today's Complex Issues* is for you.

This book is for you because I set out a few years ago to understand one of the most perplexing dynamics I repeatedly experienced in the K–12 school system: the use of deceptive behavior by school administrators. The first few times I experienced it, I chalked it up to individual personalities, the inability to speak truth to power, or poor communication. But when I began to see the use of deceptive behavior by school administrators over the years, and in a variety of settings, I began to suspect that there was much more going on than just a bit of deception here and there; I began to suspect that there was something inherent in the settings, in the complex interpersonal dynamics, in the individual notions of professional practice, or in the organizations themselves to make such a thing so pervasive.

So, after moving from the K–12 environment to the university environment, where our work is not only to teach but also to research and create new knowledge, I set out to understand this phenomenon. What you have in your hands is the result of that search: the combined knowledge, candid revelations, and, in many cases, the cathartic responses of five dedicated and experienced school administrators.

In *Ethics and the School Administrator* you will read school administrators' candid revelations about how they balance a complex array of organizational demands, interpersonal dynamics, and ethical concerns to achieve the greater good. You will read about school administrators who don't want to use deception but who also acknowledge that often they must in order to meet the needs of their students. You will read about how the school administrator's role of protecting the interests of students often conflicts with the rules of the organization. In such situations, deceptive behavior is sometimes perceived as the most humane and compassionate choice available.

When I began my year and a half of interviewing these five school administrators, I simply wanted to understand how they made sense of the use of deceptive behavior in their professional practice, but now I know this topic holds a great deal of importance as an organizational issue. Consequently, this book speaks to organizational theorists across several paradigms, and it should be of particular interest to those who are interested in educational organizations.

In addition to a tour of various organizational perspectives, the tales in this book weave together aspects of social psychology—an individual's emotional make-up, cognitive framework, past experiences, and the baggage of unresolved issues. These tales tell stories of how five school administrators made complex connections between their inner lives and their outer circumstances, especially when they found themselves in what Hennestad (1990) has called "double-bind organizational situations." In such situations, they quickly learned that organizational "truth-tellers" (Palmer, 2000) do not do well.

This is a book about the role of administrators in schools. It presents a multitude of perspectives to enhance our comprehension of the organizational dynamics that come into play when school administrators are faced with ethically compromising situations. The candid responses here not only describe individuals' professional ethics, they make an important contribution to the emerging field of leadership studies, which also is an interdisciplinary field that brings together various theoretical and historical approaches to the study of the complexities of the leadership process.

In short, this work tells the story of real people caught in crazy-making situations—and therefore provides, through a variety of research-based lenses, a revealing, scholarly, and practical examination of their sense-making processes.

I am hopeful that you will read this book and find affirmation and validation in its theoretical grounding, in the people you meet in its pages, and in the enormity of the task of running schools. I hope that teachers in educational leadership programs see the integrity of its scholarship, its authenticity of describing the realities of professional practice, and its promise for promoting lively discussions among aspiring educational leaders.

I also hope that you find here some catalyst for introspection and personal growth. During the year and a half I met with these school administrators, I had the privilege of learning from them and of asking myself about my own uses of deception. Talking with these courageous and honest people has helped me reflect on how to be a better human being in complex organizations in a confusing world. I wish the same for you.

Acknowledgements

I wish to dispel the myth that academic research is carried out in isolation and also give thanks to all the people who helped in so many ways throughout the conceptualization, writing, and completion of this book.

When I sent the first manuscript of this book to Tom Koerner for his review, he sent a kind note back to me saying that there was a great deal of merit here, but *could I make it a bit more readable.* I asked him what he meant. He said, "For example, does *every* line have to include a citation?" And, "Maybe I missed it, but what is the bottom-line message for your readers?" Tom, thank you for your kind phrasing, for your follow-up advice, and for not actually using the word "pedantic." This is a much better book because of your gentle guidance.

To make this book more readable, I asked for—and got—the excellent editorial assistance of Joanie Eppinga. Joanie not only got rid of too-dense material, tables, and charts, she created a flow that indeed made the work more readable. This book would not now be in your hands without her expert editing. Thank you, Joanie. I look forward to another project together.

I thank Al Fein for our constant and ongoing conversation about ethics, leadership, and improving the functioning of organizations, especially schools. His vantage point as an experienced school administrator and a university professor, and our many conversations about this topic, helped more than he knows.

Nancy Isaacson has been my mentor, my colleague, and my friend since 1992. Nancy's scholarship, compassion for the human condition, and constant insight continue to guide my focus and my spirit.

My colleagues at Gonzaga University continue to inspire and guide my thinking and work in many ways. Our wonderfully rich conversations in hallways, airports, and on the road provide some of the best professional development there is.

The adult students in my graduate ethics classes have been indispensable in the continued examination of organizational dynamics and the practical and professional ethics of educators. Thanks are also due to those courageous school administrators who confided their deepest concerns for your benefit. Their daily effort on behalf of their students and teachers, while faced with limited resources, political pressures, and conflicting demands, and their honesty and courage in describing the ethical compromises they are forced to choose among, makes them the heroes of this book. It is my hope that their candor will make a major contribution to the wisdom of your professional practice. Thank you, one and all. I treasure you and our time together.

Finally, I thank my wife, Scooter, for her constant generosity, good cheer, and assistance in this, and every, endeavor.

1

A Body of Knowledge

Deception is widespread, and it appears in so many different ways, and has so many effects—ranging from miniscule to fatal—that it can safely be said to be more complicated than anything else we do that carries a moral cargo.

—Evelin Sullivan

Have you, in your experience as an educator, ever found that teachers, principals, superintendents, or school board members are occasionally and intentionally less-than-honest with each other or with students? Although these individuals might have honorable intentions, their less-than-honest behavior might have negative consequences for people, as well as for the organization as a whole. Yet, the dynamics or pressures of the organization itself may well foster the perception that engaging in less-than-honest behavior is necessary.

In exploring this issue, we need to look at more than just the individual. Why, in a given situation, does someone engage in less-than-honest behavior? What role does the organization play? What are the results of the problematic behavior? Adults can always choose not to lie, so they must have some reason for doing so. The purpose here, therefore, is to explore how the very structure and nature of organizations, in this case schools, can sometimes leave individuals feeling a great deal of pressure to behave or speak deceptively. Specifically I focused on school administrators because that is the world I've experienced and because of the intensity and particularity of their positions, as they are often caught in the conflicting goals of students, parents, teachers, board members, and other school administrators at various levels in schools and school districts.

I bring to this work 27 years of experience in public and private schools, at both K–12 and higher education. This experience has allowed me to understand the language of the school culture within which school administrators operate, to ask questions pertinent to the scope of the work they do, and to be seen as an insider trying to understand the difficult decisions school administrators must make—rather than an outsider finding fault with them.

While I examine the role organizations play in deception, it is not my intention to suggest that individuals are not responsible for their actions, nor that organizations are entirely responsible for the actions of their members. Nor am I passing judgment in these pages. My goal is to explore ways in which organizational dynamics shape situations that lead to feelings of ethical compromise and less-than-honest behavior on the part of organizational members.

DEFINITION OF TERMS

Benjamin Disraeli said there are three kinds of lies: Lies, damned lies, and statistics. Throughout this book, however, *lies, lying, dishonesty, dishonest behavior, deceit, deception, deceptive behavior,* and *less-than-honest behavior* will be used interchangeably and are defined as intentional misrepresentations of the truth.

Lying can take many forms, from the simple "white lie" of telling someone her new dress is lovely when actually we think it's dreadful, to lying about serious life issues such as having an affair or stealing money. There are lies of omission and lies of obfuscation. Sometimes we deliberately imply that something is, or is not, in order to create an erroneous impression. Our reasons for lying vary as widely as do the lies themselves. For purposes of this book, I have categorized the three levels of lies that tend to be most commonly used.

The lie of *convenience* is a social lie. It is a way of appearing friendly and interested without getting involved in real conversation. Lies of convenience may be compliments or excuses. They let us interact comfortably with other people without stepping on anyone's toes.

Protective lies are more than just a social lubricant. They are designed to defend people and those they care about against the truth, and to satisfy people's own needs for approval.

Cover-up lies are those designed to hide weakness or wrongdoing and to protect the liar or the liar's group from the consequences of discovery. Cover-up lies can exist on a small or grand scale.

Most of us would agree that we have both a certain expectation of and need for honesty in our societies, for everything from being able to depend upon the accuracy of a bus schedule to feeling confident that those in positions of authority are reputable. However, few of us would condemn, for example, those who hid Jews from the Nazis and lied in the process. Truth and deception coexist and achieve differing levels of approbation at different times and under different circumstances. Plato went so far as to argue that the practice of deception must be allowed for leaders of a society.

Thus we have socially sanctioned lies, deceptions that society considers ethical for particular purposes. An example would include a nurse or a doctor telling a patient that he is doing better than his vital signs would indicate in the hope of raising his spirits, which may, in turn, contribute to his physical health. Another example would be a policeman lying to a suspect in order to apprehend him without the potentially harmful use of force. In these cases, such behavior is characterized differently from other types of lies because deceit is not the primary objective. Because the ultimate purpose is positive, society considers such deceptions to be morally acceptable.

Clearly, teasing out the difference and even the desirability of truth versus falsehood is not an easy task, yet it is worth doing because it affects us all. For this reason I have chosen to explore school administrators' feelings of organizational pressure, interpersonal dynamics, ethical compromise, and subsequent less-than-honest behavior as they relate to these dynamics.

GATHERING INFORMATION

There are many theories about deception, a good number of which come from the fields of communication, psychiatry, and social psychology. However, these fields lack purposeful connections with one another in terms of structural, individual, interpersonal, cultural, and political perspectives. Furthermore, a survey of the literature base reveals a dearth of qualitative studies on how organizational dynamics can result in deception.

Being unwilling to contrive situations to generate data (which by their very nature would promote deception), I chose instead to interview school administrators, realizing that perhaps the best way to learn about deception is to simply ask people to describe the deceptive transactions they have had with others; this method would allow me to probe for full and personalized answers to the interview questions. I selected the participants based on their membership in professional education advisory boards, as such membership is offered only to those professionals who have demonstrated excellence in their fields.

The participants were all members of advisory boards in a private university located in a metropolitan area in the Pacific Northwest. All of the participants were school administrators in public or private K–12 schools. This intact group was also chosen for the geographical, populational, and sociological diversity of the districts and schools in which they work.

Masked for purposes of confidentiality, descriptions of age, gender, years and types of professional experience, and locations and types of schools are accurately described under pseudonyms they chose for themselves. Each of the administrators had had over 20 years of experience in education. The number of years of their administrative experience, however, varied. Doc had been an administrator the longest, with 17 years. Peter had 15. Of the other three, Darlene had 5, Sandy 4, and Margot had just 1.

The interviews took place in sites chosen by these administrators, including their homes and offices, and neutral places such as coffee shops. I asked each of them the following five basic questions and additional probing questions in order to clarify answers or to get the interviewees to elaborate on what they had said:

1. Sometimes, less-than-honest behavior in organizations is not simply an individual response to a situation, but an outcome of organizational dynamics. Less-than-honest behavior can, with the best of intentions, be a result of organizational dynamics. In addition, a case can be made that less-than-honest behavior is sometimes the most humane, compassionate, and ethical way one can act. Can you give examples of this in your school or your district?

   Are there situations that unduly pressure people in your organization?

   Is the pressure ever so great that unethical practices became common?

   How common do you think such practices are?

   Are there organizational behaviors you are uncomfortable with?

   Are there times when it is too difficult to say what you think is going on?

   What do you think would happen if your organization were to be entirely honest in such a situation?

   Procedures and policies?

   Personnel issues?

   Budgeting?

   Unspoken expectations?

   Organizational image?

   The politics of the district or the community?

   Staff issues?

   Contract issues?

   Union issues?

   Has this situation changed the way you work?

2. Describe a situation in which you have benefited from or been hurt by what you believe was a less-than-honest practice of another.

   How do you think the other person justified his/her actions?

On what grounds? By what criteria?

How did you handle the situation?

Would you do the same thing to or for another person?

Were other people aware of the situation?

Did this make a difference to you? To the other person?

Do you think this type of situation is commonplace in your organization?

Would you handle the situation differently now?

Has this situation changed the way you work?

3. At times, we all have to deal with situations in our work that we find ethically compromising. Talk to me about a difficult situation in which you have found yourself, a situation in which you have felt ethically compromised, or a situation that has left you carrying a very big burden for a long time.

What kinds of situations in your job do you find to be ethically compromising?

"No-win" situations?

"Damned if you do, damned if you don't" situations?

Situations in which you are between a rock and a hard place?

Situations in which you felt you were expected to do something with which you were uncomfortable?

An area of your work that presents a very big temptation?

A situation in which you knew the simplest way to get what you wanted was by doing something with which you were uncomfortable?

A situation in which you felt bound by your position to do something you felt was dishonest or oppressive?

How did you deal with the situation?

What were the effects of the way you handled the situation?

How did things turn out?

Did you or do you have to do anything to maintain a deception?

Were others aware of how you handled the situation?

If not, would it bother you if others were aware of how you handled it?

      Would you handle the situation the same way now?

      Has this situation changed the way you work?

4. Often, while moving into a new job or a new level of responsibility, a mentor guides a protégé in adapting to the new position. Have you ever been guided, mentored, or advised regarding "the way we do things here" in a manner that made you feel ethically uncomfortable or morally compromised?

      If you were mentored, was it a valuable experience?

      If you were not mentored, how did you learn the culture of the organization?

      How did you learn to survive in your new culture?

      Who taught you what constituted a mistake in your new culture?

      Have you ever felt obligated to follow a mentor's advice with which you were uncomfortable; e.g., how to "play the game"?

      If so, how did you handle the situation?

      Would you handle the situation the same way now?

      What would happen if you were entirely honest in such a situation?

      Is there a "no talk" rule in your school/district/profession about certain topics or issues?

      Has this changed the way in which you work?

5. Is deceptive or less-than-honest behavior ever justified in your school or district?

      If so, under what conditions?

      If not, why not?

      What advice would you give to a beginning administrator?

      How do you deal with some of the multiple binds of management?

These interviews persisted over the course of a year and a half. Sometimes the administrators would call me when something especially significant was happening and we would talk. Sometimes, in their offices, there were cathartic moments. When I completed the interviews and the analysis of the data, I visited again with all of the administrators to show them the conclusions. To a person, they were happy to see such important issues spelled out in print. To a person, they were optimistic that their candor and experiences would help inform aspiring educational administrators.

Because of the professional standing and responsibilities of these administrators, and the mentoring and oversight responsibilities they hold in their position as professional education advisory board members, I made two assumptions about them. The first was that they were committed to professional integrity and had worked through a variety of issues regarding ethical compromise. The second assumption was that their commitment to their profession would help them be more likely to address the interview items with candor and more likely to share their perceptions, observations, and experiences with me. In turn, I took every safeguard to ensure confidentiality, including masking all identifying details.

I will note, however, that all the participants in this study were middle-aged, middle-class professionals, apparently Caucasians, from a Western cultural base, as am I. I mention this so that it will be understood that the conclusions drawn here are relevant to a particular population, and that similar studies of people of different socioeconomic classes, ethnicity, ages, or places of residence might garner different responses and evoke different conclusions. Finally, it is important to point out that critical differences may very well exist between schools and other types of organizations.

PERSONAL INTEREST IN THE TOPIC

As I mentioned earlier, my experience has been that teachers, principals, superintendents, and school board members occasionally and intentionally engage in misrepresentations of the truth toward each other and students. I suspect that such behavior might have been fostered by the dynamics of the organization itself. Thus, my primary interest in conducting these interviews and the reviews of the literature was to explore the relationship between organizational dynamics and experiences with ethical compromise and less-than-honest behavior on the part of administrators in the school environment.

I know my colleagues have not always been totally honest with me. I believe some of their less-than-honest behavior was designed to protect me, and I suspect some of it might have been designed to mislead me. I know I have engaged in less-than-honest behavior. I have done so both to benefit others and to benefit myself. I also know that I am now more capable of handling ethically compromising situations than I was 20 years ago.

Had I known more about organizational dynamics 20 years ago, I believe I could have dealt more honestly with various dilemmas. That is one of the primary messages of this book: We can learn from these examples and stories shared by the school administrators; we can improve our professional practice by paying attention to how these brave people worked through tough situations; we can learn to recognize the precursors to ethical dilemmas by attending to the lived experiences of these people who chose to talk about such difficult topics.

In short, I believe that a body of knowledge exists regarding organizational dynamics, feelings of ethical compromise, and less-than-honest behavior, and that this body of knowledge can be explored. It is also possible that such a body of knowledge might hold keys to increased organizational effectiveness and health.

Work is a major source of challenge, growth, and satisfaction in most people's lives, and most people do their work in, with, or through organizations. People live out many of their interests, goals, and needs through organizations. People are born in hospitals, educated in schools, spiritually guided or scolded in churches, hired to work 30 to 40 years in wage-paying organizations, diapered and fed in nursing homes, embalmed in mortuaries, looked at one more time in churches or funeral homes, and then returned to the earth. During those 12 to 20 years in schools and 30 to 40 years of work, much of who people are gets shaped, reinforced, or subtly eroded by the forces of organizational life.

Understanding the ways in which organizations shape and reinforce behavioral norms, especially the behavioral norms of deception in schools, is, I believe, a key factor of effective school leadership. Describing the ways in which organizations shape situations that contribute to ethical compromise and deceptive professional behavior can have a positive impact on organizational life. Findings from research may lead to increased knowledge in the areas of exposing and reducing destructive norms, policy formation, implementation of procedures, leadership education, and the selection of organizational leaders.

People are both better educated and more skeptical than they used to be. They know that there are often underlying and sometimes self-serving reasons behind certain decisions. It is my hope that, through this book, educators will be able to increase their understanding of the organizational, psychological, and ethical dynamics behind less-than-honest behavior in schools. I believe that such an understanding will be a step toward increasing administrative skill in leading schools and in increasing the public's trust in schools. This is why I have chosen to address a topic that has been overlooked for too long.

2

Organizations

*Lying is such a central characteristic of life
that better understanding of it is relevant to almost
all human affairs.*

—Paul Ekman

How do organizations function? This question can be addressed in a variety of ways. In the tradition of Morgan (1986) and Bolman and Deal (1991), this chapter will present an overview of organizational analysis through five lenses: a structural perspective, an individual perspective, an interpersonal perspective, a cultural perspective, and a political perspective. Although analyses of organizations are as diverse as the people who work in and study them, organizations are typically studied from perspectives that fail to acknowledge that the very same aspect of an organization can be serving a different function for different people or from different perspectives. An example from a typical elementary school might be helpful.

Schools are cultural entities rich in history and tradition. Children grow up amid the smells, sounds, and activities of their schools. Children and their parents take part in school life through all of its daily, monthly, and seasonal rhythms. Principals, superintendents, and other school administrators experience the bureaucratic portions of school life with the rituals of schedules, budgets, negotiations, job descriptions, contracts, hiring and firing, and policies and procedure. Community leaders grapple with the political complexities of finances and school board elections.

11

Schools are extremely complex organizations. Even though researchers tend to analyze organizations by placing them in categories that
make them seem more comprehensible, these divisions exist in individuals' minds only, not in the daily realities of organizational life (Morgan, 1986). Therefore, while this chapter analyzes organizations from
discrete perspectives, it's important to bear in mind the interrelation-
ships and integrated nature of organizations. Because the reality of
human interaction does not fit into five, or ten, tidy little boxes, the
five perspectives explored here are not meant to be exclusive. Rather,
each perspective enables researchers to view issues in organizations
through a slightly different lens.

CASE STUDY: WHEN A FAVOR IS NOT A FAVOR

Looking at a case study that details potentially deceptive responses to a
situation shaped by organizational dynamics is a simple way to apply
the five perspectives we will examine. The following situation, a case
study in which all identities, locations, and organizations are completely masked, will be addressed at the end of each of the perspectives
explored in this chapter.

On a Friday afternoon in October, Linda, a 40-year-old, newly hired
principal at Maple Woods Elementary, received a phone call from the
district superintendent. He asked her to represent the district at a conference to be held in Orlando regarding programs for gifted students.
He also said she could take a teacher with her. Linda was delighted at
the honor and was excited to go.

In the staff room, over coffee with Doug, the football coach, Linda
shared her news. Doug was happy for her and said she deserved the
honor of representing the district. Before leaving, Doug warned Linda
that sometimes things become a little tricky in the district, and told her
that if she ever wanted to talk about anything, he would be there for
her. Linda thanked Doug, but dismissed the comment.

Word spread quickly among other principals regarding Linda's
phone call from the superintendent. Some of them even called to con-
gratulate her. Others did not pull away from her—they just never

warmed up to her. Linda was no stranger to professional jealousy, but she did want to enjoy the company of her colleagues. Consequently, she was shocked and hurt when she heard a rumor that the superintendent had selected her for the conference because the two of them had a personal relationship. Linda knew that trying to quell such a rumor was, more often than not, counterproductive, so she kept silent.

One day the superintendent stopped by Linda's school. Some forms for the conference needed to be filled out and copied. Unfortunately, the school's copy machine was again not working. After completing the forms, the superintendent mentioned to Linda that he, too, had heard the rumors, and that ignoring them was the best approach. He said he appreciated her maturity and professionalism in handling the rumors. The superintendent left and took the forms back to his office to copy. On Monday morning, a district workman delivered a new copy machine. Surprised, Linda called the superintendent to thank him. He said cheerfully, "We want to keep our best people happy!"

Linda continued to ignore unpleasant rumors about her relationship with the superintendent, focusing instead on her work. Because her teaching staff was developing an enriched classroom program for meeting students' needs, Linda wanted to involve them in the process of deciding what teacher should make the trip to Orlando with her. She asked her staff for nominations supported by rationale statements. This process was new to the staff and they were pleased to be involved. Elaine, an African American second-year teacher who was supportive of the new program and successful in her work, was the staff's first choice. Even though the process generated some hurt feelings, especially on the part of Deb, a 20-year veteran, the written responses were clear. Linda felt good about the decision she was going to make.

Doug stopped by to see Linda, who told him about her decision regarding Elaine and the conference. Doug advised Linda to document her decision-making process, the nominations, and the rationale statements.

Linda called Phil, one of her colleagues, about another matter. Phil shared that apparently the rumor about Linda and the superintendent had grown with the delivery of the new copier. Linda mentioned Doug's cautionary comments. Phil asked if Linda enjoyed being treated well by the superintendent. Linda admitted that she did. "So, what's the problem?" asked Phil.

Two days before Christmas vacation, Linda asked Elaine to come to her office to inform her that she was the staff's choice to go with her to Orlando. Just as Elaine walked in, the superintendent phoned. He told Linda he wanted to touch base with her regarding her decision about the conference. He asked her to pay attention to the years of devoted service given to the school by specific teachers, and to the links to the community some teachers had that other, less experienced, teachers probably did not. He said he understood she would probably like to pay careful attention to those issues before making her decision and to be sure to get back to him before making any announcements.

Structural Perspective

A structural view of organizations is likely to be the most familiar perspective for most people. Simply by virtue of having gone to school and working at a variety of jobs, most people in North America have absorbed this perspective through the institutions with which they interact. Images of organizational hierarchies and authority structures are common to most people who grew up watching Mom or Dad go off to work, get raises or get overlooked, please or placate the boss, and, ideally, earn promotions before retirement.

Schools were designed with similar hierarchies. As children in school, many people learned that teachers were leaders of kids, principals were leaders of teachers, and superintendents were the leaders of principals. The structure of the workday was also clear: work, recess, work, lunch, work, and home. While adults worked for payday, students worked for grades.

A structural perspective of organizations recognizes the concerns for authority, tasks, productivity, and efficiency, as described by Taylor's (1911) scientific management theory and Weber's (1947) classical organizational theory. Taylor designed work and reward structures to meet the concern for efficiency. Weber introduced a rational, analytical method of structuring organizations.

Authority

From a structural perspective, the tasks of authority figures are clear. Leaders of organizations have to clarify and communicate organizational goals. They must create structures that include clearly understood tasks in order to ensure that the organization reaches those goals. It's their job to develop and maintain effective policies and procedures as well as clear and consistent communications that reinforce lines of authority (Weber, 1947). Ideally, they recognize that conflict arises from a faulty structure and do what they can to revise the structure accordingly. In sum, it is their responsibility to create structures that lead to increased productivity and efficiency.

Tasks

Organizations run more smoothly when they are based on predictable, routine, repetitive, and well-understood tasks. Assigning specific people to specific tasks makes it easier to define and complete these tasks (Perrow, 1986). Thus, from an organizational perspective, the roles we play in organizations are crucial. This is the "cog in the machine" approach, in which each individual's role is clearly defined and he or she is expected to play that role in specific ways, particularly in regard to duties. These roles, and the tasks that go with them, are part of the structural hierarchy (Bolman & Deal, 1991).

Productivity

A productive organization is a successful organization (Schermerhorn, 1993). Good managers establish and support the conditions needed to ensure high productivity for themselves, their subordinates, and the organization as a whole. Achieving productivity requires that an organization gets things done *and* uses resources efficiently. Problems arise when a person is wrong for the task or resources are insufficient.

The concern for high productivity requires a commitment to effectiveness and efficiency. Performance effectiveness measures whether important task goals are being achieved. Performance efficiency measures how well resources are being utilized. From a structural perspective, high productivity equals performance effectiveness plus performance efficiency.

If a person is wrong for a job, or resources are insufficient or being fought over, both theoretical and practical knowledge say that productivity will decrease. These issues affect morale. For example, principals express concern about being expected to raise test scores at the same time that federal, state, and local funding to help struggling students is cut. The lack of resources to achieve the goal leaves principals feeling powerless and unsuccessful.

Efficiency

Taylor (1911) introduced a mechanistic view of organizations. From the mechanistic standpoint, organizational structures encourage workers' perceptions of themselves as being parts of machines, whereupon such analyses as time-motion management become paramount in structuring the workday. The use of wage incentives and reward systems based on time and motion refinements, promotion policies, job ladders that emphasize greater production of simple machine-like tasks, and the transfer of valuable skills away from workers are all structural variables that affect people in organizations.

As concerned with efficiency as the mechanistic model is, tremendous inefficiencies, costs, and dysfunctions, both human and mechanical, can be attributed to the model. A structural perspective of organizations reveals that intended efficiency measures such as wage incentives and job promotions can lead to great dysfunction, as they foster competition rather than independence among workers.

A structural perspective views bureaucratic management as protecting the organization from veering off into inefficiency by ensuring that it will continue to do what it has always done. As Kanter (1983) points out, one of the problems with such consistency is that it makes it harder for the organization to improve and innovate.

From a structural perspective, then, the primary responsibility of organizational leaders is to clarify and communicate organizational goals, create a structure that will ensure that those goals are reached, develop clearly understood tasks for workers, and reward the workers who achieve those goals. Lines of authority, policies and procedures, and communications must be clear, consistent, and properly maintained if an organization is to be efficient and productive.

Structural Perspective and the Case Study

A structural perspective makes apparent direct connections from one part of the organization to another. Lines of authority and communication are clearly established and followed. In this case the lines of authority from the superintendent to the principal are clearly drawn. If Linda is not able to carry out the superintendent's directives without experiencing efficiency-decreasing tension, she may be seen as the wrong person for the job. Within a structural perspective, Linda's course of action is simple: she should choose a teacher based on the superintendent's guidelines.

A structural analyst might view the superintendent as remiss in two areas. Although he was within his line of authority in asking Linda to represent the district, he was operating outside of procedure in sending a new copy machine to her school without requiring Linda to submit the proper request. Bypassing the usual procedures in this way can be seen as favoritism, which, from this perspective, is problematic behavior. The second area in which he was remiss was in timing: The superintendent should have given Linda his directives for choosing the teacher at the time he informed her of his decision to have her represent the district. Because he did not carry out his supervisory role in a timely manner, the waters were muddied as Linda set off on her own teacher-polling strategy.

A structural perspective illustrates the inefficiencies, both human and mechanical, that plague organizations. While it has a great ability to pinpoint efficient methods, the structural perspective can also help point out the grinding and wearing away of positive interdependence among people in organizations.

Individual Perspective

Because people are *not* machines, because they have feelings, they throw wrenches into the structural works. As Schaef and Fassel (1988) point out, people, because they are human, have feelings that prompt them to make decisions different from those that the structure might require. For this reason, it is important to examine organizations from an individual perspective.

The individual perspective of organizational analysis is a broad set of psychoanalytical and medical understandings applied to people in organizations. This perspective extends beyond individual situations in which one person's behavior impacts others. Indeed, just as corporate law has expanded the view of corporations as legal entities, the individual perspective has expanded the view of organizations as living entities.

The individual perspective offers a view of what lies behind people's behaviors and dynamics as they struggle to meet their needs. It gives an observer a tool to look into, for example, a principal's constant late night work that follows a day of being obsessed with trivia. The individual perspective gives analysts a tool to examine the effect such behavior has on others in the school. Whereas a structural perspective can help an observer look at responsibilities, routines, and tasks, and make recommendations based on such an analysis, the individual perspective looks at the human element behind the situation and how that element interacts with the organization as a whole. In short, the individual perspective enables organizational analysts the opportunity "to understand the real nature of the interface between individuals and organizations" (Kets de Vries, 1991, p. 11).

Researchers who specialize in this aspect of organizational analysis examine broad areas of interaction between people and organizations: (a) human personality and relations and their effects on organizational life; (b) change and growth in adult development; (c) change and growth in career development; (d) gender issues in organizations. These four areas, relative to their potential to help understand the dynamics that might lead to less-than-honest behavior on the part of school administrators, are examined below.

Personality and Human Relations: How They Affect Organizational Life

Everyone comes from, lives in, and draws from a particular context. School administrators, like everyone else, draw upon their own personalities and experiences as they do their jobs. We have all encountered the leader who is territorial and defensive, the administrator who is charming but unable to take a stand, the authority who is intent on climbing the ladder and will do whatever is necessary to gain a promotion. Each of these types of school administrators has certain strengths, but ultimately they each have the potential to cause harm to the organization as a whole. For example, a principal with a genuine desire for harmony among the staff might cover up a problem in an attempt to avoid conflict, thereby contributing to a culture of deception.

A new administrator who is trying to buck the system and create positive change is likely to run into entrenched ways of doing things that, while dysfunctional, have become familiar to and comfortable for those involved. Experienced administrators in the district might give some feedback to the newcomer. The new person will often give up the attempt to create positive change in an effort to fit in. Thus, while personalities can affect organizations, organizations can also influence personalities.

The individual perspective sheds light on the counterintuitive process of individuals doing what they know best while having negative effects on their organizations. This perspective also illustrates the connection between individuals adapting to organizations and reinforcing existing practices of resisting change.

Clearly, the individual perspective helps organizational analysts see the human element of organizational life. Subsequently, it also helps them develop the image of an organization itself as a living entity.

Adults Continue to Grow

It is commonly accepted that people go through stages of growth and development as long as they live (Erikson, 1968). Similarly, people go through phases in their work experience. In life in general and in careers specifically, people start out with feelings of vigor and willingness to learn new things. As they mature as individuals and employees, they settle into a sense of greater competence and are willing to tackle more profound difficulties. For some, this stage is followed by a period of stability; for others, it can be a time to seek out new challenges. This is the period that encompasses the midlife crisis, in which a lack of meaning spurs people to make changes. This stage is often followed by a time of mellowing, during which limitations are accepted and people feel at peace with—or at least resigned to—what they have accomplished. Finally, there is a period of retirement or withdrawal (Baird & Kram, 1986).

Although the presentation of these four stages can look neatly clinical, the stages also hint at some of the difficulties of life in organizations. A closer look illuminates some different approaches individuals take toward their work. For example, an energetic young person entering the workplace might be expected to fit in with seasoned veterans who, through their experience, have learned that neither their behavior nor their input is going to have any significant impact on the organization (Cytrynbaum & Crites, 1989).

Men, Women, and Satisfaction at Work

Gender-based issues are both broad and deep in organizations (Lyth, 1991). Because the male perspective has long dominated organizational life, work environments have forced women to become cultural translators in order to succeed.

Whereas many men get their sense of self from success at work, the groundbreaking research of Carol Gilligan in 1982 revealed that most women feel fulfilled through strong interpersonal relationships. Women want to be treated fairly at work and they want to feel connected to those around them. They tend to make decisions based on context, rather than on lines of authority or specific rules as males are often more inclined to do. Thus, a woman might subordinate a professional goal to her desire to keep a workplace relationship running smoothly, whereas a man might be more likely to disregard the colleague's feelings in order to attain his career goal. These differences in the ways men and women find satisfaction in the workplace can point to organizational dynamics that lead to less-than-honest behavior.

Food for Thought

Do issues of personality and the behaviors of individual leaders help shape situations that lead to less-than-honest behavior in organizations? In what ways might likeable but inept administrators create situations in which avoiding conflict results in deception?

How might the stages of adult development relate to the issues of ethical compromise and less-than-honest behavior in schools? Is there a relationship between the differences in career development in which on-the-job learning of beginning principals is adversely affected by the past practices or limited interest of more experienced principals? Of the superintendent? Are experienced school administrators more likely to engage in less-than-honest behavior than less-experienced administrators?

Do organizational dynamics that reflect gender needs lead to less-than-honest behavior? For example, does a male principal's concern for success in the workplace create different dynamics from a female principal's concern for strong interpersonal connections, significant relationships, and context-based decisions? Will a female principal track and process a special request from a student or a parent differently than a male principal might?

From an individual perspective, personal, developmental, career, and gender issues in organizations can be seen as problematic. The use of less-than-honest behavior in schools might also become more apparent through this perspective.

Individual Perspective and the Case Study

Because the individual perspective offers the observer a different picture of organizations and the people in them than does the structural perspective, the needs and feelings that Linda might be experiencing now come into focus. Through this perspective, the superintendent's behaviors can be identified and labeled, the interaction between superintendents and principals can be examined, and Linda's internal responses to external events can be seen as important dynamics in the organization.

The superintendent giving Linda, a new principal in the district, a trip to Orlando and a new copier could be seen as manipulative behavior. Grooming Linda with favors can be seen as generosity that requires a payoff when the superintendent makes a last-minute demand. The individual perspective might view this superintendent as narcissistic if he feels entitled to get what he wants in exchange for the benefits he has bestowed.

Linda has received enough feedback from Doug and Phil to know that she's going to have to deal with district dynamics in one way or another. If she capitulates to the superintendent's request, Linda will be in a compromising situation: she'll be ignoring the process followed by her staff and will have to either explain or conceal her reasons for changing her mind. Whatever choice Linda makes will create problems. Certain problems can be avoided by using less-than-honest behavior, while using such behavior creates other problems.

Linda is in her midlife stage of development. She is also in her career advancement stage. The two stages have different implications. Having managed personal crises, Linda is experienced enough to weather this professional storm. Linda's career movement will depend on how she uses her personal and professional skills. Capitulation to the superintendent may indicate one career path: continued employment and the likelihood of similar experiences. Not giving in indicates another career path: repetition of similar experiences until she does give in, until the superintendent changes, or until she quits. Clues Linda has received from Doug and Phil indicate that she's not likely to have much impact on the entrenched culture of the district. Her colleagues have learned to survive and get what they want. "So, what's the problem?" said Phil. Linda has just encountered the veil covering a dysfunctional organizational norm.

As mentioned, gender issues also become more visible through the individual perspective. Female developmental theory suggests Linda will try to form strong interpersonal relationships. If she hasn't already established such relationships, they are not likely to be established now. Because of the rumors about Linda and the superintendent, complaints on her part about the bind she is in could be seen in a different context and might elicit little sympathy.

We seldom see people as they actually are—our perceptions are usually filtered through our own experiences and projections. Individual analyses of organizations provide lenses that focus researchers' perceptions beyond commonly held suppositions about people. The individual perspective helps researchers frame an understanding of human personality, interaction, and growth, and of the ways the two genders interact at work. It enables researchers to see the complexity of human interactions and their effects on the workplace in ways that other perspectives don't provide.

Interpersonal Perspective

In all human interactions, two major ingredients are evident: content and process. In most interactions, people focus on the content. Process, or maintenance, is about what happens among group members while the group is working. The interpersonal perspective examines group dynamics with respect to how well group members work together and how well they meet their goals. As Bolman and Deal say, "Both individual satisfaction and organizational effectiveness depend heavily on the quality of those interactions" (1991, p. 151). Group work can sometimes be painful, but it is the means by which much of the work of organizations is accomplished. Organizational success and individual livelihood depends on the quality of group work.

Just as individuals do, groups go through developmental stages. Tuckman (1965) categorizes the four stages of group development as *forming, storming, norming,* and *performing.* In the *forming* stage, group members check out responses of others and develop an unspoken understanding of which behaviors are acceptable in the group. *Storming* takes place when group members become hostile to one another, resisting the group structure as a means of expressing their own individuality. Conflict is high in this stage. In the third stage, *norming,* the group develops cohesion as members accept one another's personalities and characteristics. Once the group identity has been established, *performing* begins as the group becomes a problem-solving body.

Analysts focus on what goes on within the four stages in terms of process rather than content. They observe what the group is doing and how it is working. They observe how the group is handling its communication; for example, who talks to whom and how much. This perspective trains them to identify group norms—unwritten but clearly understood rules. Analysis of group process can be broken down into four main considerations: communication, leadership, influence, decision-making (Bolman & Deal, 1991; Morgan, 1986).

Communication

Communication patterns during meetings can be seen by observing interactive details such as who talks to whom and about what, how long and often members talk, and the ways in which norms and feelings influence the patterns and content of communication. Observing these elements of a group's communication pattern can reveal those members who participate a great deal and those who are more passive. An observer can also discover group norms regarding which topics are taboo, how conflict is handled, and how decisions are made. Seeing the extent to which group members trust and relate to each other is a primary purpose for observing a group's communication patterns. Obviously, communication tends to be better in high-trust situations.

Leadership

Leadership in groups is essential, but it doesn't always have to be provided by a single person. Sometimes, groups works best when the leadership role is fluid and assumed by different members at different times. Organizational researchers and analysts look for the person who performs the actual tasks, who keeps the group structured and focused, and whether these functions are balanced within the group. They take note of which figures lead and influence others. Such observations lead to another area of group interaction observed by group analysts: interpersonal influence.

Influence

In this aspect of organizational analysis, the analyst observes how group members influence one another, how power is used, and what behaviors are considered acceptable within the group. Observing these elements can reveal those members who have a lot of influence and those who are more easily disregarded, as well as the patterns of their interactions. What a researcher pays attention to regarding interpersonal influence among group members varies, depending on what the group is doing and the purpose of the observation.

Decision-Making Procedures

All groups make decisions. Some choices relate to the task at hand, while others relate to the interpersonal process. These latter decisions, such as how members communicate with each other, are usually made without the group's awareness.

Organization Development (OD) specialists use their observations about specific groups to create a comprehensive action plan, the purpose of which is to improve organizational effectiveness. An interpersonal perspective lets organizational researchers and analysts look between and among individuals and their effects on organizations; it enables them to look at the bits and pieces of face-to-face interaction that help or hinder productivity. This perspective allows organizational analysts to see the almost simultaneous process of human perception and reaction that can become habit, thereby illuminating the building blocks of group dynamics that are in place.

Another unique attribute of the interpersonal perspective is the way it views change and improvement in group performance. Organization development takes place when knowledge of group process is applied to an organization to make it more effective. OD has outcome goals with respect to the improved accomplishment of content-specific tasks, and it has process goals with respect to improving the ways in which organizational members work together.

As is evidenced by stage two of Tuckman's four stages, *storming*, the central dilemma for individuals in groups is to preserve a sense of individuality and personal identity while fitting in and participating. On one hand, being part of a group can give an individual an expanded sense of identity and the feeling of having a greater purpose. On the other hand, the existence of "mob mentality," in which people will behave far more negatively in their role as a group member than they would as individuals, has been well documented. It is this aspect of the interpersonal perspective that might be of value in exploring less-than-honest behavior on the part of school administrators.

In doing so, two questions arise: How do individual administrators maintain a sense of autonomy in the face of group norms? To what degree does being part of a group enable individuals to feel a sense of power, even to the point where they feel empowered to engage in less-than-honest behavior? Perhaps most of us have had the experience of compromising our integrity in order to retain the sense of belonging that comes with being an accepted member of a group. To fit in, individuals may withdraw into the security of the group and make decisions that they know are wrong, destructive, or dishonest.

Interpersonal Perspective and the Case Study

The interpersonal perspective of organizations can be of value in gathering information about interactions that shaped the dynamics that led to the situation Linda now faces. Such information can be of value even if the likelihood of any change effort in her district is slim. It can also be useful to organizational analysts who study the role human interaction plays in deception in organizations.

By examining her peer group, Linda could find evidence of those unstated, unwritten, but clearly understood rules of group behavior. In examining the communications among her peers, Linda could see that the communication pattern is more horizontal than vertical—that people don't talk about their interactions with the superintendent and that no one took her aside to fill her in on what kind of behavior she might expect from him. A closer examination would reveal that group norms included deal making, obliging, and secret keeping that would please the superintendent.

In examining the leadership in the district, Linda can conclude that it is top-down. The closer she looks at the leadership dynamics, the more she might see that the superintendent views himself as being in charge of tasks and that he issues directives without consulting his principals. Had he consulted his leadership team about the need for a principal to represent the district at the conference, it is possible that Linda, a newly hired principal, would not have been the one selected to go. This behavior on the part of the superintendent might explain some of the other principals' resentment toward Linda.

Observations about the superintendent's supervisory interactions are revealing when one recalls that he hinted that Linda should choose a teacher other than the one selected. This observation also reveals the possibility of another group dynamic: somebody was unhappy about either the process Linda used or the probable outcome and did not go directly to Linda about the issue. These observations indicate that group norms include unclear communication, going behind others' backs, and accomplishing personal goals by complaining rather than processing or problem solving.

In the area of interpersonal influence, the person with the greatest impact on Linda was the superintendent. Up until the last phone call, only positive things had come from him. The interpersonal perspective reveals the interpersonal exchanges that shaped the situation confronting Linda. Looking back, it is easy to spot problematic interactions. Looking ahead, the difficulty in successfully negotiating the compromising situation is also readily apparent.

Judging from her reaction to the superintendent's request, Linda was shocked. She will have to either compromise her values and professional standards, or break several districtwide group norms. The first of the group norms she will have to break, if she chooses to not follow the superintendent's advice, is to consciously not follow his implied directive. Ignoring the superintendent's wishes may lead to the breaking of a second group norm—discussing the issue with him if he contacts her regarding her decision. Linda would have to challenge a third norm to deal with feedback that could come to her from her peers, and a fourth to process the fallout from her staff.

If Linda chooses to follow the superintendent's "suggestions," then she must decide how to go about it. She could visit with one or two of her colleagues and, in an effort to adjust to group norms, ask them for guidance and find out how they deal with similar situations. She could address the issue with her teachers, many who would probably not be happy about undoing the results of their process. Linda would also have to decide how to address the issue with Doug, who clearly heard Linda state her position. She would have to decide how to process the change with Elaine. Or, Linda could simply lie. She could say, for example, that the staff results were evenly divided between Elaine and Deb, and that Deb, by virtue of her seniority and many contributions to the school, will be going to the conference.

The situation in which Linda now finds herself can be seen, through the interpersonal perspective, as the culmination of a chain of interactions that have developed into group norms and organizational dynamics. If Linda capitulates to the superintendent, she will have a difficult time doing so without conforming to destructive group norms as well. Anxiety on Linda's part could be resolved by fitting into the security of her peer group, but doing so would require that she do things she believes to be wrong, destructive, or dishonest.

This analysis of Linda's situation through an interpersonal perspective of organizational analysis is important for school administrators. It is important because it can highlight those daily interactions that develop into group norms and dynamics that then breed consequences that are difficult to avoid. It is also important because it highlights many of the precursors to ethical dilemmas that school administrators face on a regular basis.

The interpersonal perspective allows school administrators to look more closely at interactions; this is important for school administrators because such interactions often constitute the formative elements of group dynamics. Another attribute of the interpersonal perspective is that it views change and improvement in group performance as behavior that can be diagnosed, actively intervened upon, and reinforced. One limitation of this perspective is that the individual, not the group, is responsible for the change.

Cultural Perspective

The cultural perspective enables us to see the shared understandings of a group's members—its norms, assumptions, and characteristics. Physical symbols such as building design, parking access, office location, and quality of office furnishings can all reveal shared understandings of an organization's culture (Smircich, 1985). For example, in one school district's central office building, the superintendent's office might be on the top floor and have a grand view, while the Equal Opportunity Officer's office might be a cubicle next to the back door on the ground floor. Such physical symbols are not without meaning.

The schools in a particular district are likely to have their own separate and unique cultures. The climate of one particular school might include rigid structural procedures and difficult political relationships. The culture of another school might be colored by a highly emotive and personally charming, yet undermining, principal.

The shared understandings of a particular district's or school's culture show up in the way people organize themselves and their behavior at work (Bolman & Deal, 1991). Anyone doubting the reality of cultural differences among schools need only experience the role of a new-comer. Many of the understandings from the old workplace simply do not transfer to the new one. The new person will assess the new culture to learn the answers to many questions: What kind of humor is appreciated? To whom should teachers go for supplies, advice, or help? Who are the people seen as leaders or power brokers? What topics should not be mentioned in meetings? A person who chooses to ignore any of these cultural phenomena will feel another aspect of organizational culture: ostracism. This sanctioning aspect of workplace culture plays a strong role in shaping and reinforcing individual behavior.

Socialization of New Leaders

Socialization is the process wherein individuals become aware of the prevailing behavioral norms and do their best to assimilate. The culture of the work group exerts a strong socialization effect on new members. While it is assumed that people higher in the hierarchy have a greater impact on this process (Deal & Kennedy, 1982), an observant new-comer knows that a secretary or a custodian also can be influential in that such people are familiar with the organization; they know how to control access to people, information, and resources (Mechanic, 1964).

Because *Ethics and the School Administrator* is concerned with the use of deception by school administrators, it is important to examine those aspects of group culture that have a socializing effect upon them. Cultural forces have a great impact on how school administrators learn the parameters within which they are to operate.

Newly appointed school administrators tend to be culturalized products of their organization. They become socialized in terms of their approach to many things, among them the way they play their role, their interactions with superiors and subordinates, and their willingness to accommodate and strive for change (Sarason, 1972). Often, new administrators have been promoted because they have learned to be accommodating and understanding of the organization's needs; they have learned to get along and not challenge the status quo.

Relevant here is the socialization school administrators experience regarding less-than-honest behavior. Many factors affect the socialization process. Mentors, supervisors, group norms, interpersonal influences, and the administrator's own beliefs, attitudes, and values all have a shaping influence on the manner in which the newcomer fits into a new group culture. One of the dynamics I sought to understand is how the administrator responds to or interacts with the group culture in terms of less-than-honest behavior. This dynamic has to do with group norms shaped, perhaps, by mentors and supervisors, relative to norms of less-than-honest behavior.

Group Norms

People learn by observation. In the workplace, people are continually exposed to overt and covert behavior and to explicit and subtle reinforcement of their own behavior. As a result, individual learning from modeled behavior results in a set of informal rules that can govern actions, called group norms. Such norms are sometimes more influential than overtly expressed expectations.

Like individuals, groups try to develop behaviors that protect them from interference. Feldman (1985) suggests that group norms tend to develop as the result of statements by supervisors or colleagues, critical events in the group's history, precedents, and behaviors carried over from past situations. The degree to which these factors influence group norms of less-than-honest behavior, and what effects they may have on school administrators, is critical to understand if one is trying to reduce the causes of deception among administrators in schools.

Cultural Perspective and the Case Study

From a cultural perspective, we can see the socialization process Linda is experiencing as a new principal in this district. The culture of the work group exerts a strong socializing effect on new members. Linda is now feeling that effect. To the degree that she accommodates the organization and does not challenge any assumptions, she benefits. To the degree that she questions the way things work in the district, she hears disconcerting statements clearly reflecting compromise. These cultural forces have a great impact on how Linda learns the parameters within which she is allowed, or expected, to operate.

Linda is dealing with fitting into her district's culture and working through what may turn out to be ambiguity, compromise, or deception. Of the many factors that will affect Linda's socialization, those currently at play are her values, her previous experience, and the current group culture. All the forces of her new culture are going to emerge to protect the organization from interference and disruption of the status quo.

The clues available in Linda's situation relative to the issue of deception as part of the culture are the supervisory norms of rewarding compliant behavior, advance payoffs, and gratuitous compliments. Peer-group norms relative to dishonesty are the allusions to—but not full discussions of—questionable practices, and the cavalier tone and message of statements like Phil's nonchalant "So, what's the problem?"

The cultural perspective presents three images of Linda, one of which will eventually take shape. One image is that of Linda as an outsider. If Linda does not "fit in"—and the situation with the superintendent will determine to some extent whether she does—the culture will reject her like an unsuccessful organ transplant. The second image is that of Linda as an insider; all she has to do is to act consistently with the superintendent's wishes. If she does, the culture might admit her, but it will not necessarily respect her. The third image is that of a sincere reformer from the outside. In this image, Linda's individual strength and ideals are seen as a threat by the culture, and the culture will penalize her accordingly.

The cultural perspective of organizational analysis looks for common understandings around which particular groups organize their actions. Group norms are those common understandings, those informal rules of behavior shaped by the organization, or a subgroup, for group survival. Often, new administrators arrive in their positions because they have learned not to alienate themselves from decision-makers and because they have learned to be accommodating of the organization's needs; in other words, they have accepted the group's norms. These realities illustrate the possible shaping effects of organizational culture on the less-than-honest behavior of school administrators.

Political Perspective

Politics as applied to organizational life is a matter of getting one's way, influencing others, and controlling resources (Lasswell, 1958; Bennett & DiLorenzo, 1992). Operating on a political level means promoting one's interests, which involves the use of power. When power issues abound, conflict is certain to arise as organizational members debate issues, jockey for position, and form coalitions in an attempt to influence the organization's direction. As they wrestle with the separate interests of the individual members and the scarcity of resources, groups will always generate political conflict.

The political perspective offers a view different from the traditional view—that organizations are created and controlled by legitimate authorities who make sure that these organizations function in ways consistent with their formal mission and objectives. The political perspective suggests that the ongoing process of bargaining and negotiating among major interest groups ultimately determines the goals, structure, and policies of an organization. As Bolman and Deal put it, "Those who get and use power best will be winners" (1991, pp. 203–204). This is not to imply that the legitimate authorities are not also the major interest group. Rather, it is to say that the way in which power is distributed shapes the organization.

Power

Power can take many forms. It can be attributed to a person because of his or her position. It can come from within, in the form of self-knowledge and emotional maturity. It can come from the external world in the form of money, promotions, compliments, or other rewards. Power can be acquired in a variety of ways, including increasing one's popularity, gaining information, making oneself crucial to the workings of the organization, having access to people of importance, and acquiring additional skills (Bass, 1990). Ultimately, control over the behavior of others is the essence of power.

A Political Perspective of the Socialization Process in Organizations

Through a political perspective, socialization can be seen as a tool, something with which an organization can shape the world to its liking. Socialization is a resource if one controls it; it gives a person or a group power that others do not have. The notion that organizations are instruments of power, intrinsically under the control of groups or individuals, is not a comforting one. But the reality is that power is very often related to control of resources. Those who have or control the resources are more powerful than those who don't. In other words, power resides implicitly in the dependence of others.

The Purpose of Politics in Organizations

According to Mintzberg (1983), politics serves four functions in organizations. First, it allows members of a group to select their strongest people as leaders. Mintzberg explains, "Political games not only suggest who those players are but also help to remove their weak rivals from contention" (p. 202). Second, politics can ensure that all sides of an issue are fully debated. Third, politics stimulates change in an environment in which many want to preserve the status quo for their own reasons. Fourth, politics can serve as a lubricant for the making of decisions. All four of the functions facilitated by politics can contribute to the effectiveness of the group.

Political Perspective and the Case Study

Analysis of Linda's situation through a political perspective builds upon the other perspectives insofar as it explores the usually hidden element of power. The political perspective explores the issue of power in personality, ambition, group dynamics, communication, and group norms. As mentioned earlier, promoting one's interests is the primary element of operating on the political level. This understanding makes it clear that the superintendent will likely be reliant on politics if he is to assert his agenda, because in his work with the school district, politics is a matter of getting his way by influencing others and controlling resources. The link between the supervisor's control of resources and getting his way is apparent in Linda's situation.

If Linda maintains her own preference of taking Elaine to Orlando, conflict is inevitable. In this type of conflict, power will become a key resource. The political perspective would examine the power Linda brings with her to the situation. It is evident that Linda is not, at the moment, part of a strong coalition. Rather, she is caught between two strong power bases: the superintendent's interests and Deb's on one side, and the majority of the school's teachers and their interests on the other. In her position, Linda might have to purposively *choose* the power base with which to align herself. The political perspective suggests that because those who acquire and use power will be winners, Linda might align herself with the coalition that would give her more power and greater access to scarce resources.

Linda has no advantage over the superintendent with regard to her position. If she had been in the district long enough and had achieved significant goals, she would have some degree of personal power from which to operate. As things stand, if Linda intends to take issue with the superintendent's wishes, she will have to join, or build, a coalition. She will have to draw upon her teachers' sense of her as a strong leader who can survive this battle.

If Linda cannot achieve this, she will not be able to successfully stand up to the superintendent; she will not be able to uphold the process she used and the outcome it generated; she will not be able to take Elaine with her to the convention in Orlando; and she will not be seen as a strong leader. She will be forced to capitulate to the superintendent and compromise her role and relationship with her staff.

Of course, Linda does have the option of telling her staff the truth. She could say to her teachers, "I'm sorry, but I've been told to use a different method of choosing the teacher who will go with me. I assure you, it's nothing personal about who was or was not chosen. Rather,

I've been told I failed to pay attention to certain criteria with regard to this decision." In one respect, such a statement might get Linda off the hook, as it would keep her from having to actively lie.

In another respect, such a statement might create more problems for Linda. Her staff might go from believing that Linda was the best thing that ever happened to Maple Woods Elementary to thinking, "The superintendent got to her, too." Such a change of heart among her staff could strongly affect Linda's future at the school.

Linda's teachers are still in the process of forming their image and expectations of her. In this formation stage, the teachers have high expectations of change and will give Linda more allowances for change now than they will by the end of the school year. If Linda fails to take advantage of that now, she may not get another chance. From the political perspective, capitulating and appearing weak at this point will irreparably hurt her image as a leader of change.

Studies show that the majority of Americans believe their elected leaders consistently lie to them (Bok, 1979). Much of the public knows not to judge many leaders' statements by their veracity, but rather by the extent to which they promote the interests of the leaders. If this is true, Linda's teachers could probably correctly read the subtext of any apology or explanation Linda might make. And they could probably, because of their experience in the district, read between the lines and know that the superintendent had influenced Linda. Linda's teachers would be likely to see her as having been fully socialized into the district's leadership team. From a political perspective, it appears that Linda has been skillfully maneuvered into a no-win situation. It appears she will have to learn to play the game or get out of it.

SUMMARY

This chapter has shown that organizations don't operate out of any single set of driving principles. School districts, schools, and the people in them operate from driving forces that can best be understood from a variety of perspectives.

Schools and school districts are not democracies composed of individuals with equal influence. However, just because these organizations are not fully democratic does not mean that individuals should be ignored. Nor, on the other hand, does it mean that individuals should have no influence on the organization outside regular and legitimate channels. Because legitimate authority usually favors a single, dominant view, the use of political influence might be the only way to broaden discussion and challenge old assumptions.

As you will see in chapter 5, the school administrators involved in these interviews will help us get in touch with aspects of organizational reality that are often very hard to talk about. Indeed, they may even contribute to what LaBier (1986) refers to as conditions of *modern madness*, to which the most successful professionals are extremely vulnerable. These administrators ask us to consider just what constitutes "normal" responses to organizational situations which require repeated uses of deception by leaders in order to make things work and to protect human beings.

Why is this important to know? Because it is in meeting the needs of individuals and groups that power and politics come into play, and power and politics present all levels of school administrators with ethical dilemmas—thus difficult choices—in how to meet the needs of their students.

3

Behavior

There is a distinction between a person who tells a lie and a liar. The former is one who tells a lie unwillingly, while the liar loves to lie and passes his time in the joy of lying.

—Harry Frankfurt

Just as understanding how complex organizations, such as schools and school districts, work requires examining them through a variety of perspectives, so too does understanding the complex behavior of the human beings in these complex organizations.

This chapter presents, in the tradition of Sears, Peplau, and Taylor (1991), the basic theories used in social psychology to understand behavior, especially theories that have proven to be useful in understanding conscious choices to use less-than-honest behavior.

Why social psychology? Because important changes have taken place in social psychology, thanks to accrued research and knowledge. Also, because we are concerned with understanding school administrators' *conscious choices* to use less-than-honest behavior, which is addressed by social psychology, and not the sociopathic or compulsive use of deceptive behavior (in which neither logic nor ordinary emotions serve as foundations of behavior) which is not. For the purpose of studying deceit in the complex organizational life of schools and districts, social psychology provides a great starting point because it emphasizes factors in organizational situations that generate the same general response from most people.

The major theoretical approaches in social psychology include learning theories, cognitive theories, motivational theories, decision-making theories, social exchange theories, and role theories. Each of these perspectives emphasizes one aspect of the causes of behavior without claiming that the other perspectives are unimportant or irrelevant. Another contribution of social psychology is its integration of ideas from the classic theoretical traditions of the past: psychoanalytic theory, behaviorism, and Gestalt psychology.

OVERVIEW OF MAJOR THEORIES IN SOCIAL PSYCHOLOGY

Social psychology is the scientific study of social behavior. It considers how *most* people perceive and respond to others and how they are affected by social situations. Social psychology is concerned with uncovering the answers to questions regarding how and why we perceive things the way we do, why some people are helpful to others, why some people are entirely honest with others, and why some people engage in less-than-honest behavior.

Although many other fields study social behavior, what makes social psychology helpful for understanding why some school administrators might choose to use less-than-honest behavior is that it is distinct in its approach. Some fields, such as sociology and anthropology, use the societal level of analysis, which would help us understand broad, cultural phenomena. Psychology uses the individual level of analysis, which would be better suited to understanding the individual complexities of compulsive or sociopathic lying. But social psychology uses an *interpersonal* level of analysis, which will help us understand specific instances of the use of deception in a variety of school-based settings.

Social psychologists focus on people's current social situations, environments, attitudes, and behaviors, and the context within which these elements interact. A social psychologist would ask probing questions: What is it about an individual and a particular situation that would make a person more or less likely to obey a supervisor's orders? What aspects would make a person disregard the orders or behave deceptively in response to the orders? In broad terms, what aspects of any immediate social situation are likely to determine human behavior? In trying to understand the use of less-than-honest behavior by school administrators, social psychologists would ask what kinds of interpersonal situations lead to an increase in less-than-honest behavior.

Blending the interpretations of behavior from the sociological, psychological, and social psychology perspectives is worthwhile if we are to fully understand complex social behavior. Considerable overlap exists among disciplines in the kinds of studies that are undertaken to understand complex human behavior. The single question "What causes less-than-honest behavior?" can be answered in many ways.

Historical Roots of Social Psychology Theory

In attempting to explain human behavior, social psychologists draw upon a variety of theories. Before discussing current theories in social psychology, it is useful to consider some of the historical roots of the field.

In the early 1900s, pioneer psychologists developed three major theoretical perspectives in the field of psychology. They are psychoanalytic theory, behaviorism, and Gestalt psychology. These three theoretical perspectives have left their mark on contemporary social psychology and are part of the mental models social psychologists use to understand less-than-honest behavior. Following is a brief discussion of these three theoretical perspectives and their relevance to the present study.

Psychoanalytic Theory

Freud (1913/1953–1966; 1915/1961), the founder of psychoanalytic theory, proposed that human behavior is motivated by powerful internal drives and impulses such as aggression and sexuality. Freud believed adult behavior is shaped by unresolved psychological conflicts that can usually be traced to childhood experiences.

Psychoanalysts try to understand the conscious and unconscious inner forces that drive human behavior. They tend to characterize an individual's deceptive behavior as being symptomatic of unresolved psychological issues. The psychoanalytic perspective can be helpful in understanding individual behavior in organizations, as well as in understanding responses to organizational dynamics. The psychoanalytic perspective often tends to characterize individual responses as pathological.

Behaviorism

Behaviorism, developed by Pavlov (1927), Watson (1919), and Skinner (1938; 1953; 1957; 1959; 1963), focuses strictly on observable behavior. Behaviorists are not interested in subjective thoughts and feelings. Behaviorists study only what can be directly observed and measured. They also examine ways in which the environment shapes behavior, and they suggest that current behavior is the result of past learning. Because behaviorists examine how the environment influences behavior, their perspective is valuable in looking at the possibility that organizational dynamics shape situations that lead to less-than-honest behavior.

Gestalt Psychology

The branch of psychology known as *Gestalt*, from the German word for shape or form, was developed primarily by Köhler (1929), Koffka (1929; 1953), and Lewin (1935; 1936; 1951), who focused on the ways "individuals perceive and understand events and people. From this perspective, people see the environment as a whole consisting of more than the sum of its parts. They do not perceive situations or events as created from many discrete elements, but rather as dynamic wholes" (Sears, Peplau, & Taylor, 1991, p. 6). In examining the possibility that organizational dynamics shape situations leading to deceptive behavior, a gestalt perspective allows for the consideration of psychological issues, the ways the environment shapes behavior, and the ways people make sense of, and operate in, the world.

It is generally agreed that the problems studied by social psychologists are too complex to fit any one of these three general theories of behavior. The value of these models to social psychology research, however, is clear. Social psychologists recognize, through psychoanalytic theory, that behavior is influenced by personal motives and by emotional reactions. Behaviorism reveals the ways in which previous learning can shape current behavior, and the ways in which experience can shape attitudes and behavior. Gestalt psychology is seen in the contemporary emphasis on social cognition, the study of how people perceive and understand their social world.

Contemporary Theories in Social Psychology

As stated earlier, major contemporary theories in social psychology are grouped in the following six categories: learning theories, cognition theories, motivation theories, decision-making theories, social exchange theories, and role theories. The following overview is not intended to be comprehensive, but rather intended to compare and contrast the elements of the six categories that can illuminate this study. To help create a clear comparison, each approach is applied to the same specific illustration of less-than-honest behavior. The following situation, a case study in which all identities, locations, and organizations are completely masked, will be addressed at the end of each of the perspectives explored in this chapter.

Case Study: Ambiguity and Distrust

One Saturday morning, Mike, a fourth-grade teacher, went to his classroom to catch up on some work he'd been unable to do because of administering standardized tests that week. After entering the school, Mike noticed Wendy, the principal, in her office, pencil in hand, examining answer sheets from students' standardized tests. As Mike neared the office, he saw Wendy erase some filled-in answer bubbles on a sheet and then fill in two different bubbles. Mike assumed that the sheet was a cover sheet for the school's tests. He walked into Wendy's office to say hello. Mike then saw that the paper was not a cover sheet, but a student answer sheet. Wendy looked shocked to see Mike, and she quickly mentioned the need to clean up stray marks on student answer sheets because the office personnel did not have time to do it.

Unfamiliar with the practice of anybody reviewing, let alone handling and erasing marks on student answer sheets, and being a little suspicious of Wendy's reaction, Mike did not believe Wendy's explanation. Unsure of how to respond, Mike simply commented about working on Saturday and quickly went to his classroom.

Later on in the same school year, school district test scores were published in the local newspaper. Students in Mike's school traditionally scored near average in most subject areas. This year, however, his school's scores were well above average in all areas and were now the highest of all 27 elementary schools in the district. Mike suspects that this gain in test scores is a result of Wendy changing student answers. Wendy knows of Mike's suspicions. Because of her school's success, Wendy has been asked to provide consultation to other schools in the district on how to improve their test scores.

Learning Theory

Learning theory, long the dominant approach to understanding behavior, suggests that a person's current behavior is shaped by past experience and learning (Bandura, 1977). Learning theory holds that in specific situations, people learn certain behaviors which, in similar situations, become habits. This approach to understanding human learning usually aims to explain a person's specific behaviors instead of a person's psychological state of mind.

Learning theory would attempt to explain less-than-honest behavior, such as Wendy changing student test responses, as a learned and overt act, not an act in response to a subjective internal state. Learning theory would look to the current environment in seeking causes for this overt act. It would emphasize the models of behavior to which a person has been exposed. Learning theory suggests that the socialization process in Wendy's profession might provide examples for imitative behavior. Deception might appear to be the best way for Wendy to achieve certain professional goals.

Cognitive Theories

Cognitive theories of social psychology maintain that "behavior depends on the way people perceive the social situation" (Sears, Peplau, & Taylor, 1991, p. 9). This perspective comes from the work of gestalt psychologists. Two of the core beliefs of the cognitive perspective (Lewin, 1935; 1936; 1951; Aron & Aron, 1989) are that people are prone to grouping and categorizing the things they perceive, and that people focus attention primarily upon things that stand out. Cognitive theorists believe these two tendencies result in our attempts to bring meaning to how we feel, what we want, what kinds of people we are, and basic issues of that sort.

Unlike learning approaches, cognitive theories focus on current perceptions rather than on past learning. They emphasize the importance of an individual's perception of a situation, not the supposed reality of the situation. Individual interpretation is the determining factor behind an individual's behavior.

According to Cody, Marsten, and Foster (1984), it takes more thought to create effective deceptive messages than to tell the truth. To develop believable lies, deceivers must first construct messages that are consistent with existing facts and can pass as plausible substitutes for the truth. Furthermore, subsequent messages must be closely monitored to ensure they are consistent with the original lie and that they can plausibly extend and clarify the lie and other related statements around the lie.

Such research suggests that if Wendy altered the original test scores and lied to Mike, she must now maintain that lie. Wendy might need to alter next year's test scores as well. Maintaining the lie will require more cognitive effort on Wendy's part to make sure subsequent messages are consistent with her original lie. To maintain the lie and create consistent follow-up messages, Wendy might have to explain why she needs extra time to privately review answer forms, resulting in further lies.

Motivation Theories

Another approach to understanding behavior looks at individuals' motives. The psychoanalytic view of motivation described by Freud emphasizes the importance of powerful innate drives (especially those associated with sexuality, aggression, and unresolved childhood conflicts), whereas social psychologists are more likely to consider a greater and more diverse range of human needs and desires. Motivational theorists contend that people's needs influence their perceptions, attitudes, and behaviors (Kelley, 1967; Weiner, 1986). For example, to enhance her professional status and satisfy a need to be seen as successful, Wendy might alter students' answers and take credit for the resultant rise in test scores.

To understand Wendy's behavior in changing students' marks, a motivational perspective would try to uncover her reasons for doing so. Was she changing marks based on a need for approval, or for a sense of success? Was she motivated by a district reward structure linking increased pay to increased test scores? Was Wendy motivated by fear of not having her contract renewed if students at her school did poorly on the test? A motivational analysis might go further to try to identify ways in which Wendy's environment fostered the particular motives that led to the changing of student marks.

The essential characteristic of deception is the motivation to deceive effectively. Generally, people prefer to tell the truth unless they have a reason to do otherwise (Nyberg, 1993; Ekman, 1992).

The decision to lie is often accompanied by a considerable motivation to do so effectively. Deceivers usually understand and weigh the consequences associated with detection. The negative consequences of being caught in a deception far outweigh the consequences of being truthful. For example, a principal who falsifies student responses on answer sheets will probably face a more severe punishment for the deception than for having low test scores.

In other situations, deceivers are motivated by the possibility of achieving positive outcomes that are less likely if the truth is told. For example, school principals may exaggerate the effectiveness of test-score improvement activities to enhance their professional appearance or to increase their chances for promotion. Research suggests that the greater the consequences, the greater the motivation to deceive effectively (DePaulo, Kirkendol, Tang, & O'Brien, 1988).

Motivations for lying vary with gender. According to Justice (1987), women's motivation for deception tends to be stronger in the areas of avoiding hurt feelings, protecting a third party, avoiding interaction, and avoiding causing someone worry. Men's motivation for deception tends to be stronger in the areas of refusing requests, making excuses to get out of doing things they're supposed to do, and getting things that they want. These differences largely reflect and reinforce gender role stereotypes, indicating that deception strategies may be part of gender socialization.

It is commonly understood that pretty much everyone tells white lies. These small deceptions are the only type of deceit that most people willingly admit to, because they are regarded as socially acceptable and are not thought to do severe damage. It turns out that lies are used most often to benefit the self in one way or another. According to Camden, Motley, and Wilson (1984), the primary motivation to lie is to save face.

These findings from motivation theory studies in deception may relate to Wendy's case in intriguing ways. If she has indeed lied to Mike, has altered original test scores, has achieved district recognition for improved test scores, and must effectively maintain the lie, the negative consequences of discovery are increasing at a phenomenal rate. Wendy now has an additional motivation to lie: avoiding embarrassment.

Justice's gender-difference findings seem to not apply in Wendy's case. Wendy's deception does not fall into the categories described by Justice as typical of women's motivation to deceive: avoiding hurt feelings, third-party protection, avoiding interaction, and avoiding causing another worry. Rather, Wendy's motivation appears to be one more commonly ascribed to males: getting what she wants in terms of career advancement.

Decision-Making Theories

Decision-making theory maintains that people calculate the outcomes of their actions and then pursue the action they perceive to be the most reasonable (Sears, Peplau, & Taylor, 1991). In Wendy's situation, she might believe her only other option is to wait for the actual test results; if they prove undesirable, she would need to develop a schoolwide program for increasing test scores. Wendy might think she cannot afford to choose the option of spending a whole year diverting teacher and student attention to test scores.

Through almost all perspectives of social psychology, deception can be seen as a planned strategy. Having knowledge about people, situations, and likely consequences permits people to anticipate events in which deception can be seen as an alternative that, for whatever reason, is preferred to the truth. As a principal who has the knowledge of procedural timelines, student ability, and curricular issues in her building, Wendy has likely had at least the opportunity to think about her situation, make some decisions, and plan her deception. The fact that she might have altered test scores in her office on a Saturday, rather than in the privacy of her home, might suggest an overall decision-making strategy. The application of these findings to the case study suggests that if Wendy did engage in such a highly planned activity, her deceptive messages could contain fewer verbal and nonverbal clues to her deception and could be difficult to detect.

Social Exchange Theories

Social exchange theorists do not focus on the behavior of the individual, but rather on behavior in a relational context. The central idea in this theory is that as people interact with each other, they engage in a cost/benefit analysis. People may sometimes engage in this process in a planned and rational way, but even when they do so unconsciously, the process of interacting with others creates rewards or benefits such as approval, status, and financial gain; and costs such as loss of status, loss of work or money, and disapproval for those involved (Sears, Peplau, & Taylor, 1991).

For example, future interactions between Mike and Wendy might be expected to become more stressful because of Mike's information about Wendy. Wendy might experience tremendous costs if Mike reported what he saw. On the other hand, Mike might now have a great ally in Wendy if he does not report his observations. It might greatly benefit Wendy to benefit Mike.

Role Theories

The term *social role* refers to the set of norms that apply to people in a particular position. Social psychologists have taken two approaches in analyzing social roles. One emphasizes social structure and the other emphasizes interaction processes (Sears, Peplau, & Taylor, 1991).

The social-structural approach emphasizes how individuals might "play out preexisting scripts" (p. 14). This perspective tends to be more useful in formal settings, such as the workplace, where role definitions are more likely to be more detailed and specific. In Wendy's case, a role analysis might consider her membership in various groups and what the group expectations are for her behavior.

The interactionist approach emphasizes the processes of role-making through which individuals actually create, modify, and redefine their roles during the course of their interactions. This approach views people as actively creating and revising their own scripts and defining their own characters. Wendy had to decide which parts of the test were important, which students' forms to alter, and when and where to do the erasing and changing. Her choices were guided by her knowledge of how well students typically do in certain subject areas, which students were the likely low-scorers, and where the safest or most convenient place to do this work would be. This view would recognize the considerable freedom Wendy had to choose her actions, unlike other views that see "people as relatively passive actors playing out their assigned roles" (p. 15).

The leadership skills of role-playing and convincing others of sincerity are placed by some researchers in a category labeled *self-monitors*. Polished statesmen and political leaders, called *high self-monitors*, can act like social chameleons, capable of adapting their interaction style to the constraints of particular situations. High self-monitors are adept at interpreting and responding to social cues and are highly concerned with maintaining socially appropriate behavior. Low self-monitors, on the other hand, are those individuals who are generally content to be guided by their own beliefs about the interaction.

Keating (1993) suggests that a strong relationship exists between dominance and deception among men. For both children and men, there is a direct relationship between the ability to lie convincingly and leadership skills, especially in the areas of problem-solving and convincing others of something that may or may not be true. However, no such relationship appears to exist for women.

Another interesting point of Keating's work is that children and adults who score high on deception skills are also able to control their facial and body displays. People who are able to control their body language are seen by group members as having the greatest leadership abilities.

These findings are especially significant to the case study. If Wendy had been able to successfully alter student test answers and parlay the false test results into increased visibility in the school district, we could conclude that Wendy fits in the category researchers call high self-monitors. Individuals in this category of leaders have shown themselves to be skilled in conveying sincerity and matching their interaction styles to the constraints of specific interactions. If Wendy fits in this category, she might have been demonstrating such leadership skills. If so, Wendy's case is an exception to Keating's findings that no significant relationship exists between women who lie and women who emerge as leaders.

Also interesting are Keating's findings that describe a link among deception skills, controlling facial and body displays, and being seen by others as a leader. The finding that this connection exists in both children and adults, and is especially strong in males, is intriguing. The notion that apparent sincerity can influence people's perceptions of leadership is interesting in terms of this book's examination of the interpersonal dynamics of the school administrator's role.

SUMMARY

This examination of ethical compromise and less-than-honest behavior in schools had the same goals as current social psychological research:

to explore a familiar topic (deception), to generate initial hypotheses about this common experience of social life, and to do so through the appropriate scientific methodology. This overview of social psychology theory supports the thesis that people do not operate out of any single set of driving principles—cognitive, emotive, or experiential. It also supports the idea that people tend to operate from a variety of driving forces that combine emotions, learned reactions, cognitive aspects, and elements of unresolved issues from the past. To dive into such a variety looking only for learned behavior is to ignore the gestalt. To look only for emotional responses is to ignore cognitive processes.

4

Ethics

How can I say anything that'll make you feel better if I'm not allowed to lie to you?

—Dean Koontz

What are people really like? What makes people operate the way they do? What happens when people face difficult options and do things they do not believe in? Examining ourselves—why we do what we do—is the very essence of human psychology . . . and of ethics. The study of ethics, from the work of Plato 2,400 years ago to the contemporary work of Downie and Telfer, constitutes a rich tradition in both human psychology and philosophy.

The purpose of this chapter on ethical decision-making is not to illustrate the difference between right and wrong, but to show how school administrators might choose among ethical approaches to decision-making as they face the difficult choices they must make every day. When school administrators face difficult and ethically compromising situations, it is not always a simple task to weigh the issues of right and wrong, of ethics, of justice. Most of us like to think of ourselves as just and ethical people. However, to be just and ethical, people need to know something about the demands of justice and how they apply in their own circumstances. What is fair? What is just? How do we decide? These are the central concerns of the ethical theorists presented here.

This chapter applies five major theories of ethics to the issue of ethical compromise and possibly less-than-honest behavior within a school-based context. The five theories of ethics are representative of the work of six major theorists: Plato, Hume, Kant, Mill, and the joint work of Downie and Telfer. Each of these theorists makes a significant contribution to, and represents a distinctly different position in, the continuum of ethical theory from the tradition of Western philosophy. I chose these five perspectives of ethics for three reasons. First, they form an identifiable core of the Western tradition of philosophy and ethics. Second, they present a broad historical overview of the development of ethical theory. Third, these five theories represent a continuum of ethical decision-making typologies that can be used to identify the manner in which school administrators make ethical decisions.

None of these philosophers spoke specifically about the binds of middle managers, the budgetary or political pressures facing superintendents, about the personality-based problems school administrators face on a daily basis, or about the practical and professional ethics of school administrators. None of them spoke directly to the issues of managing a negotiated contract, which students should be exempted from standardized tests, or accounting for differences in student achievement and conduct. None of these ethical theorists spoke directly to the issue of dealing with negative cultural norms, the subtle messages from mentors, or the quid pro quo agreements between the central office and the school. What they did speak to, however, are the basic concepts that have proven to be helpful in considering such difficult decisions: justice, sentiment, reason, benefits, respect.

The remainder of this chapter is organized around three components:

1. A case study describing an ethical issue
2. Analysis, application, and assessment of five theories of ethics
3. Summary assessment of the five theories.

CASE STUDY: PROFESSIONAL OBLIGATIONS, PERSONAL RELATIONSHIPS

The following situation, a case study in which all identities, locations, and organizations are completely masked, will be addressed at the end of each of the perspectives explored in this chapter.

This example of possible ethical compromise involves Joe, the administrator of a residential treatment center for acting-out adolescents. Joe is faced with a situation in which a staff member, Howard, has had sexual intercourse with a teen-aged resident, Crystal, who is now pregnant, will soon turn 18, and will then be released. Howard and Crystal have told Joe that they are in love and plan to marry. The ethical issue is whether Joe should report the incident as required by law, or refrain from reporting the incident because these two individuals seem to be acting out of love for each other. Other concerns Joe faces include providing responsible management for his school and protecting his school's reputation.

While it is clear that there are other ethical issues apparent in this case study, namely the roles and behavior of Howard and of Crystal, these will not be addressed, because, while they are important, they are not relevant to deception among school administrators.

The ethical issue under consideration in this analysis is that of Joe's responsibilities and choices in the handling of this situation. As the administrator in charge, Joe has a variety of social, organizational, and legal responsibilities. Joe has responsibilities to the youngsters in the treatment facility. He has responsibilities to the staff members and caseworkers in the organization, and responsibilities to uphold the laws of the state. Joe also is accountable to the board of directors of the treatment center for managing the organization in a businesslike and discreet manner.

The rulers of the state are the only ones who should have the privilege of lying either at home or abroad; they may be allowed for the good of the state.   —Plato

Plato's Ethics

Because the concept of justice is central to most theories of ethics, this chapter begins with Plato's theory, in which he develops a definition of justice and places it directly in the center of his framework of ethical decision-making.

Plato was deeply concerned with justice, especially as it relates to decisions made by leaders. He defined the concept several ways in his *Republic* (380 BC/1974), ranging from "justice is to perform one's own task and not to meddle with that of others" (p. 98), to "justice does not lie in a man's external actions, but in the way he acts within himself. He does not allow his soul to meddle with another" (p. 107). In the *Gorgias* (385 BC /1987), Plato talks about justice in a manner approximating a contemporary legal definition: "Justice: Proper administration of laws. In jurisprudence, the constant and perpetual disposition of legal matters or disputes to render every man his due" (Black, 1991, p. 599).

For the purposes of this chapter, justice can be defined as "right conduct toward others through due process of the law." This definition encompasses doing one's own work, not meddling with the work of others, and ensuring that every person is appropriately recognized and compensated.

In the *Gorgias*, Plato contended that the pursuit of justice is most admirable because it provides "either the most pleasure, or benefit, or both" (p. 46), and that "what a man should guard himself against most of all is doing what's unjust" (p. 49). Plato also argued that education and justice are the primary determinants of happiness.

Regarding the pursuit of justice, Plato believed that one should know justice before practicing leadership, so as not to say things merely to please the crowds. Plato believed the craft of caring for the soul was the most important of all, and that true leaders had the responsibility of practicing that craft. The craft of caring for the soul could not be practiced without the knowledge of justice.

Looking further into his theory as it relates to right action and the use of power, Plato wrote, "If a person does anything for the sake of something, he doesn't want this thing that he's doing, but the thing for the *sake* of which he's doing it" (p. 29). From this position, he maintained that if a just person were to punish another justly, that punishment was done because it was a good thing, a better thing to do than to not do. Plato then asserted that committing an unjust act is a greater evil than being treated unjustly: "So, because it surpasses it in evil, doing what's unjust would be more evil than suffering it. Injustice, then, . . . and all other forms of corruption of soul are the greatest evil there is" (pp. 33–45).

Plato spelled out his definition of *unjust* very clearly in his *Republic*: "We have shown that it is never just to harm anyone" (p. 10). Thus, if an action harms someone, it is unjust. Plato also stated in the *Republic* that injustice makes an individual incapable of achievement because he is at odds within himself and is not of one mind; he further notes that injustice makes any organization incapable of achieving anything.

It is important to note that in *Gorgias* Plato asserted that all forms of corporal and capital punishment, sentenced justly, as authorized by law as punishment for unjust behavior, would be just punishments carried out for the benefit of the person. Plato, the idealist, believed that pain and suffering were the only ways "to get rid of injustice" (p. 109), and that one's soul undergoes improvement if he is justly disciplined.

Plato believed that there are corrupt conditions of the soul, and named among them cowardice, ignorance, injustice, and lack of discipline. He argued that injustice, and doing what is unjust, are the greatest evils, and that paying a debt for them is what gets rid of the evil. Plato believed that the full and proper administration of justice, in that it gets rid of injustice and indiscipline, is the greatest benefit of all.

In an analysis of Plato's theory, justice can be defined as right conduct toward others through due process of the law. Any action of a person that causes harm to another person can therefore be labeled unjust. Committing the evil of injustice makes individuals and organizations incapable of achieving anything worthwhile. Finally, one must pay for, or be punished for, the evil of committing an unjust act.

Plato's Ethics and the Case Study

In applying Plato's theory to the case study, it is important to point out that schools, and their administrators, are governed by state law.

Any violation of these rules, standards, or principles is, in effect, a violation of the law, and would be considered by Plato to be unjust. Among the laws to which school administrators are responsible is generally one in which the state asserts the right to intervene in order to safeguard the general welfare of children. In this law, provisions are made for the reporting of information to appropriate public authorities about cases of neglect and abuse of children. It identifies all people required to report actual or suspected instances of child abuse, which include institutional personnel. Any violation of this law generally constitutes a misdemeanor.

Clearly, Plato would hold that school personnel are obligated to carry out all legal requirements. If Joe were willing to violate administrative and civil law for the purpose of what would appear to be protecting his position and income, he would be hurting other people and perpetuating a system that harmed the people in it and the people it intends to serve. Plato would hold that such an administrator would be acting out of cowardice, and that he would be serving his interest of position over his responsibility of justice and due process toward others. Plato would maintain that ignoring due process hurts innocent people, that doing so to maintain personal position is unethical and a great evil, and that it would result in the organization's being "incapable of achieving anything" as a unit.

Assessment of Plato's Ethics

From Plato's arguments in the *Gorgias* and the *Republic*, five key components of his theory of ethics, especially as they relate to the administrator's ethical dilemma in the case study, can be identified:

1. Justice can be defined as "right conduct toward others through due process of the law."
2. Any action a person takes that causes harm to another person can be identified and labeled as unjust and unethical.
3. Doing an unjust act is evil and unethical.

4. Injustice on the part of individuals or organizations makes them incapable of achieving anything.

5. Individuals must pay for, or be punished for, the evil of doing an unjust act.

It is clear that Plato believed that the quest for truth and justice is critically important. Plato's theory supports the pursuit of what is best for everybody, and that "what is best for everybody" is comprised of right conduct toward others, for without attention paid to right conduct toward others, life becomes a scramble for limited resources with only a few in control.

Plato held that to do an injustice to another person is a great evil, and that it damages one's own soul as well. One point of Plato's theory, that no good can come from the administration of one who does unjust things, supports the notion that unjust acts move individuals and organizations toward corruption. Once people start hiding evidence of wrongdoing, where do they stop? Once colleagues and subordinates see that one has a choice about whether to follow the law, who decides which laws to uphold or when to uphold them? What message would such actions send to the residents of a treatment center?

Plato's idealist arguments about absolute truth and justice are, simply put, the thin line between totalitarianism and anarchy. Are they applicable to the practical and professional ethics of school administrators? Plato's theory of ethics might well be paraphrased: The quest for ultimate truth and justice is a worthy and necessary pursuit, because in the end, without it, anything goes.

That honesty is the best policy, may be a good general rule; but it is liable to many exceptions. —David Hume

Hume's Ethics

The Scottish philosopher David Hume attempted to show that utility and agreeableness, and nothing else, are the values at the root of ethics. In his *An Enquiry Concerning the Principles of Morals* (1751/ 1983), Hume argued that ethical judgments are really judgments about what people consider to be virtues and vices, and that ethical judgments can be derived through observation of what *is*—through the observation of what people do and what they value.

Hume's theory is sentiment-based and denies that there are any ethical facts. He wrote, "Truth is disputable; not taste. What exists in the nature of things is the standard of our judgment; what each man feels within himself is the standard of sentiment" (p. 14). In his philosophy, Hume defines virtue to be "whatever mental action or quality gives to a spectator the pleasing sentiment of approbation; and vice the contrary" (p. 85). Hume wouldn't necessarily condemn any particular action; the same action might be wrong in one situation and acceptable in another. This is what constitutes the "flexibility" in Hume's theory of ethics.

Hume listed virtues that he believed every culture valued. Among these was self-interest, which Hume argued is both a valuable part of nature and compatible with interest in others. Building on this idea, he came up with the notion of "enlightened" self-interest, meaning that one does not pursue one's interest to the detriment of others. Hume presupposes that justice is based on community moral values, and that it must emerge out of shared community values.

To Hume, *utility* is the sole origin of ethical behavior and justice. He explained, "The rules of behavior and justice depend entirely on the particular state and condition, in which men are placed, and owe their origin and existence to that utility, which results to the public from their strict and regular observance" (p. 23).

Hume equated justice with the way people relate to one another regarding property rights, with "property" meaning real property and "social goods" as well. Regarding the practice of justice, the regulation of property or social goods, he explained, "We must be acquainted with the nature and situation of man; must reject appearances, which may be false, though specious; and must search for those rules, which are, on the whole, most useful and beneficial" (p. 28).

Hume argued that one's obligation to obey laws is founded on nothing but the interests of society. He also held that the various consequences of any practice are, on many occasions, doubtful, and subject to inquiry. Hume believed that the object of municipal laws is to fix all of these questions with regard to justice, and that an accurate sense of judgment is often required to give the true determination "amidst such intricate doubts arising from obscure or opposite utilities" (p. 83).

Hume believed that justice is absolutely requisite to the well-being of mankind and the existence of society. Regarding the virtue of justice, Hume argued that the benefit resulting from it is not the consequence of every single act, but, rather, arises from the consequence for the greater part of society.

Hume's Ethics and the Case Study

As Hume proposes, the practice of justice is the search for the most useful and beneficial rules for society, and that people are obligated to promote society's best interests. Although serving one's self-interest is not wrong, it should not take place at the expense of other people.

Hume believed in the practical application of reason. He believed that sentiment, or feelings, provided the goals, but he also believed that reason and judgment help people reach those goals. Regarding the current case study, Hume would acknowledge that "obscure and opposite utilities, various interests" are seemingly at play, and that "an accurate sense of reason or judgment is often required" to manage this issue.

Regarding the issue of the administrator in a residential treatment center, concerns arise as to how to handle the situation from Hume's theory of ethics. The appropriate behavior of all staff members is one issue; the safety and well-being of the abused youngsters in their care is another. Staff members displaying appropriate modeling for the resident teenagers is a third issue. Hume might argue that for Joe to choose not to intervene in this situation would be to act in disregard for the best interests of society.

On the other hand, Hume could contend that the specific illegal activity might not be of such great concern under certain circumstances. For example: Suppose Crystal and Howard really were in love with each other; suppose they really did plan to marry once she turned 18. Would justice be served in making an issue out of the situation? Would not, perhaps, the best interests of all be best served by letting the dust settle, and letting Howard leave his employment with the residential treatment center without being charged with any crimes? Here is an entirely different situation, one that is not so defiant of, or threatening to, society's laws. In this slightly different view of the issues in the case study, the need for Joe's intervention and action is not so great.

Hume identified a host of virtues that he claimed people hold dear and use to blame or judge people and their actions. Among them are justice and courage. In looking at this case study, Hume might view Joe as lacking in both courage and justice if he were to fail to report his findings to the appropriate law enforcement agency. Failing to intervene in socially dangerous behavior is evidence of lack of courage.

Furthermore, given the norms of professional ethical behavior, Joe's first obligation is to the students, the residents, in his charge. This means protecting them from harm. Joe clearly has the obligation to put the needs of his charges first. If Joe carries out these responsibilities, he will have demonstrated the pursuit of justice and demonstrated the virtues of discretion and prudence. If Joe fails to carry out these obligations, what lack of moral virtues does he display? A few come to mind: decency, justice, honor, prudence, courage. Hume acknowledged that various outcomes and utilities are difficult to sort out; he does, however, offer a clear picture of Joe's moral obligations.

Assessment of Hume's Ethics

Hume believed that people's emotion determines their goals, and that rationality helps people achieve their goals. This last point separates Hume from other earlier philosophers who held a deep-seated distrust of human emotions. Hume believed that benevolence spans cultures and that no one would deliberately hurt another. His theory, however, is based on his assumptions, his generalizations, and his interpretation of his observations, and he trusted that it all fell into a good schema. It is possible that some of Hume's assumptions lack an internal consistency and that some of his generalizations are incorrect.

Hume acknowledged the difficulty of weighing the various utilities and outcomes inherent in many situations. He expressed an innate trust in people's ability to use their reasoning and judgment to sort things out. In many instances, however, the outcomes of actions are beyond the ability of mankind to reason out ahead of time. People do not always know where their actions will lead, so it is in the best interest of all people to act with regard to future generations, not just present-day society.

Regarding the case study, would it be permissible to ignore Howard's behavior if he and Crystal did marry? Would it be less permissible to ignore Howard's actions if they planned on living together? Could ignoring Howard's behavior prove to be correct regardless of the laws and consequences? Would it matter if the residential treatment center were located within walking distance of New York's Central Park . . . or in a remote area of the Mississippi Delta?

This concern for the future implies some system of moral behavior that goes beyond the immediate pleasure or displeasure provided to society. Were we able to trace some current malady back to an action of an earlier time, and then travel to that time to make the displeasurable outcome known to the one who acted, would we be able to claim the act to be an immoral one? If not, why not? Would Hume claim a statute of limitations on the morality or immorality of actions? If so, what is it?

These questions make it difficult to disregard the timetable question. When people consider their "greater happiness," do they consider just their circle of friends, or do they extend their consideration to their city? Do they stop at their city, or do they extend their consideration to the nation or the world? Do they cease their considerations with their generation, or extend them to future generations?

The issue of the timetable of outcomes as measures of ethicality of actions is a difficult one to make sense of or respond to in a temporal reality. It is unclear whether Hume gave adequate attention to the "greater happiness" of society. He argued:

> While we are ignorant, whether a man were aggressor or not, how can we determine whether the person who killed him, be criminal or innocent? But after every circumstance, every relation is known, the understanding has no farther room to operate. . . . The approbation or blame, which then ensues, cannot be the work of the judgment, but of the heart. (p. 85)

If people limit their approbation or blame, if people limit their "work of the heart" to only the present, do they not then disregard the past and fail to learn from it? If people fail to learn from the past, do they not then fail to grow more sensitive to the greater happiness of society? And do they not then fail to make any consideration for the well-being of society in the future? A Platonic analysis, a Christian analysis, or even an internally consistent interpretation of Hume's theory of ethics would present a vision of a self-shaping society spiraling into collective disregard for anything outside of its sense of its own greater happiness. This concern for a bias-free perspective implies some system of moral behavior that goes beyond the immediate pleasure or displeasure provided to society.

In freeing himself from the heavy-handed religious authoritarianism of his day and making use of the trend of scientific observation, Hume created a system for examining the ethicality of individuals' decisions and actions. A troubling aspect of Hume's theory is that an action might be ethically acceptable in some situations, but not in others.

Some of the reasoning and application of Hume's theory is practical. Situations do exist in which, once all the evidence has been gathered, a person's behavior can be seen to be free of malice, or the result of ignorance and misunderstanding. The very same act committed by one who did it with the intent to harm another can be a more serious situation. What becomes evident, from this example, is that the appropriate application of Hume's theory requires a person to act from a position of reason and experience.

Another troubling aspect of Hume's theory is his belief that the ethicality of a decision is based on its outcomes, which may not be known for years. To compound this problem, the outcomes may vary at different times. People's sentiments regarding an action and its outcome may vary widely for years after a decision has been made.

Because people cannot always see to the end of their actions, they must act with prudence and a positive regard for the future. This is the use of reason and compassion, and a high moral regard for more than mere convenience or present-day utility. Hume's theory argues that society indeed shapes itself toward what he holds to be universally valued virtues.

If one sees society's perceptions of benefits to itself as culturally and temporally bound, and therefore not adequate measures of morality, Hume's ideas become problematic. His theory is perhaps most useful as a description of how he believes people *do* make moral decisions, not a philosophy of how people *should* make moral decisions. In this regard, his theory offers little in the way of providing guidance for the difficult decisions people must make in life. Hume's description of the way people do make moral decisions is, however, appropriate to the question of why school administrators might choose to engage in less-than-honest behavior.

I ought not to lie even though lying were to bring me not the slightest discredit. —Immanuel Kant

Kant's Ethics

Kant's theory of ethics was developed in response to Hume's emotive theory of ethics. Kant's is a rational theory, in that a priori reasoning is the basis for his categorical principles. In *Grounding for the Metaphysics of Morals* (1785/1981), Kant states that "the ground of obligation here must therefore be sought not in the nature of man nor in the circumstances of the world in which man is placed, but must be sought *a priori* solely in the concepts of pure reason" (p. 12). Kant argued this point on the basis that logic cannot have any empirical part, that logic and universal laws of thought cannot be based solely on experience. His reasoning was that the laws of nature are based on what *does* happen, and the laws of ethical philosophy are those according to which everything *ought* to happen.

Kant states that if a law is to be ethically valid, it must carry with it absolute necessity and it must apply to all rational beings. Kant grants that rules based on empirical grounds can be called practical rules, but never ethical law. He states that ethical philosophy gives a priori laws to humans as rational beings, and even though humans are capable of pure practical reason, it is not so easy to make that idea effective in the day-to-day reality of life.

Kant asserts that morals "are liable to all kinds of corruption as long as the guide and supreme norm for correctly estimating them are missing. For in the case of what is to be morally good, that it conforms to moral law is not enough; it must also be done for the sake of the moral laws" (p. 3). Conformity to moral law is only contingent and uncertain because the nonmoral ground may produce actions that conform with the law, but that also produce actions contrary to the law. From this point, Kant sets out to establish the supreme principle of morality.

Kant contends that the only thing that can be regarded as good, without qualification, is good will. In direct refutation of Hume, Kant explains, "A good will is good not because of what it effects or accomplishes . . . it is good only through its willing, i.e., it is good in itself" (p. 7).

Kant then develops the idea that existence of reason has a more worthy purpose than providing for happiness:

> [I]ts true function must be to produce a will which is not merely good as a means to some further end, but is good in itself. To produce a will good in itself, reason was absolutely necessary, inasmuch as nature in distributing her capacities has everywhere gone to work in a purposive manner. (p. 9)

Kant here reveals his image of people as beings of nature with wills that are naturally good, who have the power of reason to guide the will toward good itself; he also contends that reason can lead people to things greater than mere happiness.

Kant presented three propositions of morality. The first one states that "an action must be done from duty in order to have any moral worth" (p. 12). The second contends that "an action done from duty has a moral worth independent of anything that is attained by that action, that the principle of volition itself has the moral worth" (p. 13). The third says that "duty is the necessity of an action done out of respect for the law" (p. 13).

Thus, the obligation exists to act in such a way that one would be willing to have one's own rules of practice made into universal principles that would apply equally to everyone. This is known as Kant's *categorical imperative*.

Kant has led us to a place where actions can be judged as ethically permissible, or impermissible, by their relation to duty. Regarding duty, he says, "Duty is the necessity of an action done out of respect for the law" (p. 14).

Kant identified four basic duties, two of which he identified as "perfect" duties, or those that permit no exception in the interest of one's inclination. His two examples of "perfect" duties are the duty to maintain one's life and the duty to keep promises made to others. The "imperfect" duties, or those that allow some discretion as to the allowance of one's inclination, are the duty to cultivate one's talents and the duty of beneficence to others.

Kant argued on behalf of the dignity and worth of all humans:

> Rational beings are called persons inasmuch as their nature already marks them out as ends in themselves . . . which are thus objects of respect. . . . Now morality is the condition under which alone a rational being can be an end in himself, for only thereby can he be a legislating member in the kingdom of ends. . . . Thereby he is free as regards all laws of nature, and he obeys only those laws which he gives to himself. Accordingly, his maxims can belong to a universal legislation to which he at the same time subjects himself. (pp. 35, 40–41)

Developing further the idea of autonomy of the will, Kant argued that the "autonomy of the will is the property that the will has of being a law unto itself" (p. 44), and that the principle of autonomy is basically to choose in such a way that "in the same volition the maxims of the choice are at the same time present as universal law" (p. 44). Concluding the argument on behalf of free will and autonomy, he argues, "What else, then, can freedom of the will be but autonomy, i.e., the property that the will has of being a law unto itself?" (p. 49).

Kant's Ethics and the Case Study

In examining the ethical issues that emerge from the case study, it is important first to acknowledge that Kant would not be in favor of judging another person. He would expect people, as autonomous beings, to be much more interested in examining their own behavior. In addition, to fully understand another's behavior, one would have to be able to know that person's maxims. The rule of universality as the sole means by which to assess the ethicality of decisions or actions leaves no room for interpretation and can appear simplistic.

The first ethical issue to confront is that of acting in regard to Kant's duty of being of benefit to others. Although it is impossible to get inside of Joe's head or fully understand his maxims, Kant's categorical imperative can be used to examine Joe's behavior. Kant could argue that if Joe were to ignore Howard, Crystal, and the rest of the residents of the treatment center, he would be treating them as means toward his own end (such as protection of his career), which is ethically impermissible.

In addition, as an educational administrator, Joe must carry out certain obligations such as those spelled out in professional standards of behavior, including making the well-being of students the basis of all decisions and fulfilling professional responsibilities with integrity.

Kant would maintain that in cases where civil law and moral law overlap, civil law supports moral law. He would also see that "duty is the necessity of an action done out of respect for the law" (p. 13). Therefore, Joe has the obligation to meet these duties of professional behavior. If he were to ignore civil law and these duties, Joe would have shown that he failed to keep the promises he made when he swore to uphold the standards of his profession and that he failed to be of benefit to others. Joe's actions would also hurt the children in his organization and they would hurt the credibility of other administrators in the organization.

If Joe were aware of any practices that were illegal, he would have the responsibility to report any violations to the proper authorities. By using the test of universality, such action is seen to be categorically imperative. If Joe's actions were of good intent, such intent constitutes acting out of duty, which is the highest form of good in Kant's theory. To be commendable, an action has to be undertaken for the right maxim, namely, respect for moral law. In addition, as an autonomous being, Joe is responsible for judging his own motives.

Assessment of Kant's Ethics

Kant cleared the way out of the situational bog that characterizes Hume's theory. Where Hume argued that the ethicality of an action is based on its societally beneficial outcome, Kant said that if a law is to be ethically valid, it is to be valid as a ground of obligation, it must carry with it absolute necessity, and it must apply equally to everyone.

Kant argued that the ground of obligation has to be sought neither in the nature of people nor in the circumstances of the world in which people are placed, but solely in the concepts of pure reason. In addition, he believed that virtue lies in the intent or maxim of an action, not in the action itself. Kant offers rational proof of a stable ethical foundation. He presents a way to build upon that foundation through categorical imperatives and the test of universality.

Kant believed in conscience. He pointed out that people are able to recognize whether their actions are motivated out of honest or dishonest intent, out of respect for ethical law, or out of self-interest. Kant's philosophy brings clarity and specificity into the process of decision-making. According to Kant, if something is a rule for one person, it is a rule for everyone. There is no private morality. There are no private rules or exceptions that hold for some people and not others. So, in this case, in asking himself "What if everyone were to do what I am about to do," Joe can easily see whether that choice is the right one . . . or not.

It is confessedly unjust to break faith with anyone: Like other obligations of justice, this one is not regarded as absolute.   —John Stuart Mill

Mill's Ethics

In *Utilitarianism* (1861/1979), Mill was looking for the middle ground between Hume and Kant. He acknowledged that there are two ways of looking at ethics: the inductive and the intuitive approaches. After discussing the merits and pitfalls of the two approaches, Mill sided in favor of the inductive approach—he was indeed an empiricist, and believed in using the data from reality and inductive reasoning to arrive at principles of ethical behavior. According to a utilitarian view of ethics, actions are right in proportion as they tend to promote happiness, wrong if they tend to produce the reverse of happiness; pleasure and freedom from pain are the only things desirable as ends. Mill argued on behalf of an empiricist approach, using inductive reasoning:

What is there to decide whether a particular pleasure is worth purchasing at the cost of a particular pain, except the feelings and judgment of the experienced? When, therefore, those feelings and judgment declare the pleasures derived from the higher faculties to be preferable in kind ... to those of which the animal nature ... is susceptible, they are entitled on this subject to the same regard. (p. 11)

Mill's utilitarianism never sanctions self-benefit at the expense of society. Mill explains, "The happiness which forms the utilitarian standard of what is right in conduct is not the agent's own happiness but that of all concerned" (p. 16).

Mill's utilitarianism made the greatest break with other theories of ethics in arguing that when judging an action, a motive is of no value. However, Mill believed that the motive *does* have a great deal of value when looking at the worth of the person. Mill made another strong argument on behalf of an empirical approach to ethics in acknowledging that people have a vast background of experience and knowledge to draw upon in making ethical decisions.

The existence of a conscience, to Mill, was "a feeling in our own mind; a pain more or less intense" (p. 27), and the sense of conscience was the result of the way a person is taught. He contended that the ultimate sanction "of all morality is a subjective feeling" (p. 28).

Mill argued that freedom of choice holds enormous benefits for society, that one's own private interests count for no more than the interests of others, and that altruism is beneficial to society.

Mill defines justice as a sentiment by saying that justice is a utility:

We have seen that the two essential ingredients in the sentiment of justice are the desire to punish a person who has done harm and the knowledge or belief that there is some definite individual or individuals to whom harm has been done ... the idea of justice supposes two things—a rule of conduct and a sentiment which sanctions the rule. The first must be supposed common to all mankind and intended for their good. The other (the sentiment) is a desire that punishment may be suffered by those who infringe the rule. ... [Justice is] a name for certain classes of moral rules which concern the essentials of human well-being more nearly, and are therefore of more absolute obligation, than any other rules for the guidance of life. (pp. 46–58)

Finally, Mill states that "justice remains the appropriate name for certain social utilities which are vastly more important, and therefore more absolute and imperative, than any others are as a class" (p. 63). Mill presented his theory of utilitarianism not as a theory endorsing expedient practices, but as a theory of ethical behavior devoted to the pursuit of happiness for all, one that appeals to the native sense of conscience. Mill's utilitarianism never sanctions self-benefit at the expense of society.

Mill's Ethics and the Case Study

Mill would argue that Joe should examine the entire scenario and take whatever action would produce the most desirable result for society. As an administrator, Joe would need to examine his primary responsibilities, which clearly fall on behalf of the abused and neglected youngsters under his care.

According to Mill's philosophy, it would be Joe's primary responsibility to provide children with the treatment and the modeling that most effectively leads them toward healthier decision-making in their own lives. What is the best way to accomplish that end? By using the modeling and enactment of justice and fairness, Mill would contend.

Did Howard have a right to have sex with Crystal? No, he did not, because Crystal was a minor, and she was in treatment. Given the age differential and his positional power, Howard took advantage of Crystal, no matter how willing Crystal was.

Crystal and the other residents in the institution need to know that Howard had no right to do what he did and that no one should be victimized. They need to see that Howard receives the legal consequences for his choice of behavior. Mill would argue that it is Joe's job to see to it that all of this happens.

If Joe were to ignore the situation and let Howard and Crystal do whatever they choose, he would be seen as causing a great deal of anxiety and discomfort for the youngsters in the treatment center. By ignoring his responsibilities, Joe would be causing a great deal of pain for society which will soon be absorbing these youngsters.

Mill's utilitarian theory makes Joe's decision easy for him. For the benefit of the greatest good, Joe must report Howard's actions to the appropriate agencies. Howard must receive the legal consequences for his behavior. The abused adolescents must see that adults are not above the law, and they must be helped to see that the treatment center really is advocating on their behalf.

Assessment of Mill's Ethics

Although Mill's theory of utilitarianism is often criticized for its perceived expediency, it can also be viewed as providing a variety of benefits. First, it is pragmatic and makes use of common frames of reference. Second, when applied as Mill intended, the theory insists that the greatest benefit of society, not one's own personal benefit, is of primary importance. Finally, Mill's description of justice allows more regard for the different and less precise applications of justice than does mere civil law.

The simplicity and pragmatic nature of Mill's theory, however, is offset by one great weakness: its relativity. The morality of an action, under Mill's theory, is determined by relative criteria. The greatest good must be quantified from a variety of possible outcomes and points of view before an action can be determined to be the appropriate one to take. This approach presents problems similar to those described in the assessment of Hume's theory, in that the morality of an action is based on its outcomes.

The "flexibility" of Mill's utilitarian theory of ethics is somewhat less problematic than is the "flexibility" of Hume's emotive theory of ethics, due to Mill's ideal of utilitarianism. Mill's theory of ethics is still problematic, however, because of its lack of firm criteria by which people can judge the ethicality of their actions.

The fundamental principle governing private or public behavior is respect for human nature.   —Downie and Telfer

Downie and Telfer's Ethics

In *Respect for Persons* (1969), Downie and Telfer present a theory of ethics that synthesizes the key elements of the four theories discussed so far. Their theory can be summed up as follows: Respect for persons is the single fundamental principle from which all rules of ethics are derived.

Downie and Telfer begin with the notion that "the idea of the individual person as one of supreme worth is fundamental to the ethical, political, and religious ideals of our society" (p. 9). They refer to Kant's and Mill's philosophical works as examples in which this idea is given a central role. Downie and Telfer hold that people are intrinsically valuable in and of themselves. They contend that what is worthy of respect in a person is the ability to exercise rational will in self-determination and rule-following.

Downie and Telfer deal with Mill's utilitarianism by saying that "it is unintelligible to suppose that happiness matters without supposing that the people whose happiness is in question matter" (p. 39). They believe that the "principle of liberty may conflict with the positive aspects of utility. These positive aspects stress the importance of achieving the maximum satisfaction of interests, and for this to be possible some degree of social co-operation is necessary" (p. 57). This position requires an understanding of liberty that has both a positive and a negative side, with the negative side consisting of refraining from interference in people's pursuits of their aims and in not causing them pain or distress.

Downie and Telfer state that people have basic duties to themselves to develop their human nature, called *duties of private morality,* and contend that in developing natural talents, a person is fulfilling the requirements of private morality. They form a symmetry between respect for others and self-respect by arguing that self-respect is to private morality what respect for others is to public morality. This argument is based on two premises: first, that if people take respect for others to be equivalent to respect for themselves, the sense of *self* in both cases is the same; and second, that the sense of *respect* is the same in both cases. Downie and Telfer hold that public and private morality are not two moralities, "but two aspects of a single fundamental moral principle" (p. 84).

Downie and Telfer's Ethics and the Case Study

Respect for persons as the ultimate principle of morality makes the proper course of action for Joe clear. Downie and Telfer would argue that moral rules exist and provide safe ethical guidance. These ethical rules exist because people have learned by experience that certain types of action are liable to have consequences which are either good or bad. Is it right for a staff member to have sex with a youngster in his charge? No. Would it be right for Joe to ignore such an event? No. Is Joe obligated to follow the legally prescribed actions if it occurs? Yes. Downie and Telfer would contend that Joe should report Howard to the proper authorities for Howard's sake, for Crystal's sake, and for his own sake.

Assessment of Downie and Telfer's Ethics

Downie and Telfer have successfully synthesized a theory of ethics based on Plato, Hume, Kant, and Mill. They have incorporated the concern for reason that exemplifies the idealistic and rationalistic theories of Plato and Kant. They have taken into account the feelings critical to the emotive theory of Hume. They have paid attention to the virtue ethics of Plato and Hume, and have retained the principles of Kant's and Mill's theories. The strength of Downie and Telfer's theory of ethics is not its originality, but the skillful interweaving of its underlying principles.

The single greatest conflict in Downie and Telfer's theory is that because both duty to self and duty to others are binding, one must sometimes choose between the two. The authors answer this problem to a degree in their discussion of self-referring morality. Basically, they contend that if morality is to be self-referring, it involves a kind of respect, which means maintaining autonomy or self-control. This approach seems to move in the opposite direction from Hume's theory, in which exists the problem of not being able to look far enough into the future to assess the consequences of an action. With Downie and Telfer's theory, people can look to the here and now for evidence of self-control, and to respect for others as guides for ethical decision-making.

SUMMARY

The concepts of justice, sentiment, reason, benefit, and respect have been explored and described for centuries. These concepts were analyzed in the preceding section and reveal a broad range of ethical principles. They form a continuum of concerns people must face in making difficult decisions.

The intent of this chapter is to articulate the wide range of ethical bases and to show how different concerns and conceptualizations of justice can play out differently with regard to the same organizational situation. Different aspects of ethical decision-making theories were explored in order to interpret how individuals deal with issues of ethical compromise and the decisions they make. This chapter shows that not all ethical bases are the same, and that a variety of ethical theories can be used by people in order to make difficult decisions.

As you will see in the following chapters, and especially in chapter 5, the administrators who participated in these interviews did not advocate less-than-honest behavior or the use of deception; in general, they maintained that the subject was highly undiscussable. Their candid responses do, however, suggest that the requirements of the school administrators' position conflicted, both ethically and in terms of goal accomplishment, with the *professional role* of the school administrator. Less-than-honest behaviors, then, became one of the mechanisms by which these individuals rectified this predicament of role conflict. As honest as they were through the year-and-a-half-long interview process, we can still only guess at the true personal costs these choices must continually require.

5

Organizational Politics

The great enemy of truth is very often not the lie—deliberate, contrived, and dishonest—but the myth—persistent, persuasive, and unrealistic.

—John F. Kennedy

The interview responses from the school administrators are examined from the perspectives of the three broad theoretical frameworks presented in chapters 2, 3, and 4: organizational theory, social psychology theory, and ethical decision-making theory. Therefore, presentation of the responses and summary of the findings are divided into three parallel chapters. Chapter 5 examines the interview responses from the five perspectives of organizational theory. Chapter 6 presents those responses from the six perspectives of social psychology theory. Chapter 7 presents the analysis through the lenses of five theories of ethical decision-making.

This chapter begins with a short biographical description of each participant. All responses were excerpted verbatim from the interview data and were sorted into broad categories. Themes were then generated on the basis of the categories and their properties. Because some excerpts fit into more than one category, they are listed in more than one category. The interview responses show how school administrators' conscious use of deception emerged as a result of situations shaped by various dynamics in their schools and districts.

Each section contains an explanation of the responses and concludes with a summary of the findings, and each of these three chapters concludes with an overall summary of the findings from the organizational analysis, social psychology analysis, and ethical analysis, respectively.

Descriptions of Participants

Five school administrators who formed an intact group, based on their membership in one of four professional education advisory boards at a private university in the Northwest, participated in this study. They are employed in a variety of school districts.

Margot had been in education for 25 years. Although it was noted that all the participants appeared to be Caucasian, in this case appearances were deceiving. Margot comes from a family of color and says, "I just didn't get the dark skin." Margot says her ethnicity is a part of who she is, and that her ethnicity makes a difference in her life.

Sandy had been in education for 22 years, Darlene for 29 years, and Peter for 26 years. Doc had been in education for 30 years. Doc is of southern European ancestry, so, though technically Caucasian, he has darker skin than most whites. He says, "In school I was the only child who had the coloring I have. I used to get as mahogany-colored as this desk. It made me realize all the discrimination of being poor, of being a different color."

Because the interview responses, their meanings, and the patterns they formed were my focus, identification of the participants by name is not a feature of this book beyond this point.

Structural Theory and Findings

As discussed in chapter 2, a structural perspective of organizations highlights lines of authority, official lines of communication, detailed job descriptions, policies and procedures, productivity, effectiveness, and tasks. Because of its focus on organizational efficiency, not human needs, the structural perspective is likely to reveal the inefficient or procedurally difficult elements of schools and school districts. From this perspective, the main reasons the school administrators engage in ethical compromise and deception have to do with (a) their roles as administrators, (b) the resources available to them, and (c) the rules they are obligated to follow.

Roles

The participants said that deception results primarily from their wanting to influence decisions, protect children, maintain productivity, and obtain and protect resources. Influencing others turned out to be a significant factor in the school administrator's role. For example, one participant spoke of not having any say in who transfers into her building. As a result, if she did not expect to find working with the potential transferee to be satisfactory, she might be strategically ambiguous in describing the open position in such a way that might discourage the potential transferee from coming to her school.

A second role, that of protecting children, also creates ethically compromising situations for school administrators. For example, a participant reports her use of differential treatment of certain children in her attempt to protect them from being placed in Behavioral Intervention (BI) or Developmentally Impaired (DI) classrooms and from being labeled as BI or DI students. She knows the standards and the cutoff lines are the same for all students, but says she "might not let a particular student get to the line because that is a big label to carry around." The analysis of the data through the structural perspective illustrates that meeting children's needs might compel some administrators to feel they must go beyond specific rules.

The pressure to be effective in terms of producing high statewide standardized scores also contributes to deception among school administrators. One participant explained that a way to relieve the pressure might be "to deny kids the opportunity to take the tests. There would be opportunities to take tests for kids, throw out certain tests, and make some kids ineligible."

In describing the school administrator's role of obtaining and protecting resources, participants reported that the need to protect resources under certain circumstances, given particular rules or expectations, can lead to difficult ethical compromises. Such ethical compromises can result in manipulating district enrollment forms, hiding money in school budgets under alternate categories, and misrepresenting actual vs. budgeted amounts.

Resources

The protection of resources is significant to most of these school administrators. They identified time, money, and personnel as commodities they would go to great lengths to protect.

A common response regarding the protection of the resource of money was: "There's one item on the school budget I find I have to hide, and that's my own personal travel." Also typical is this participant's indication that he purposely limits access to his budget process and masks actual budget categories and amounts in order to avoid conflict and to protect his budget from the scrutiny of specific people. He reported that his district does the same thing with interest money from bonds and that, by doing so, his district is able to use that interest to fund other priorities.

Time is another highly valued resource. A typical response from one participant was that she would manipulate the reporting of children's enrollment in school in order to provide more aide time for her teachers. She also said she might tell her staff that she knows neither an answer to a specific question nor how she intends to approach an issue—when, in fact, she does have an answer and does know what she is going to do—in order to provide more thinking time for herself.

The well-being of teachers is a resource administrators want to protect. One participant described the deception involved in trying to have students and their parents believe that schools and teachers can be all things to all children. He said, "We haven't done a good job of letting students and parents know that they have unreasonable expectations in that they expect every teacher to get along with every kid. That is just not going to happen. We haven't done a good job of letting them know that we have limits and that they have to live within the limits."

Other responses regarding the protection of teachers and other organizational resources include a participant's acknowledgment that she relies on the use of nondisclosure to avoid telling students all of the facts, because she knows that her teachers could not handle the task of dealing with 1,500 students. For example, she doesn't advertise the flexibility she allows some students with regard to PE credits because she knows there is no way she could deliver the same flexibility to all of her students. Nor is she confident that her counseling staff of five can provide an adequate guidance program for all 1,500 students. So, she protects her teachers and the school through the use of nondisclosure.

Rules

The participants identified the rules they might ignore in order to meet the needs of students and teachers. They said district policies and guidelines were not as important to them as getting students into, or keeping them out of, certain programs. They explained that they would ignore program qualification rules to serve students and would use differential treatment to keep students from qualifying for programs. Regarding rules for necessary but unqualified services, a typical response about students who need—but do not qualify for—certain services, was: "I would, without a doubt, ignore policy and procedure. We'll pick them up as part of our caseload because they fit, we can schedule it, and we agreed as a team to serve their needs. I have no problem serving them."

These school administrators all found that a contradiction exists between toeing the line bureaucratically and meeting people's needs. As one person expressed this common sentiment, "Meeting people's needs is more important than following the rules; I run risks regularly with human factors."

Clearly, some administrators engage in less-than-honest behavior, including protecting resources and bending rules, in order to protect their students and staff. This analysis of the data through a structural perspective shows that the participants identified the less-than-honest behaviors in which they engaged as:

1. Hiding funds
2. Manipulating procedures
3. Ignoring policy
4. Using nondisclosure
5. Forging
6. Creating, on their own, new rules to address particular situations.

INDIVIDUAL THEORY AND FINDINGS

Whereas a structural perspective can help us view roles, resources, and rules, the individual perspective looks at the human element behind situations. Because the individual perspective of organizations is psychological in nature, it gives us the opportunity to understand what happens when people and organizations come together. From the individual perspective, the administrators' responses reveal that their personal (a) characteristics, (b) experiences, and (c) beliefs and values were key factors in how they made their ethical decisions.

Personal Characteristics

Three items were identified as major elements of these administrators' personal characteristics relating to ethical discomfort and less-than-honest behavior: candor, compromise, courage. The individual perspective, applied to their comments, shows that candor can alleviate the tension involved in ethical compromise and deception.

The concern for candor, and the nature of its role, becomes clearer upon examination of who might be served by hiding behaviors or breaking rules. The components of candor appear to be the need for openness, the need to talk through issues, and the need for feedback. The concern for candor, it seems, has to do with self-regulation, not self-protection.

Compromise appears to be a response to conflict that makes administrators somewhat uncomfortable. They varied significantly regarding what they were willing to compromise. For example, one participant said she would not allow a particular student to transfer to another high school, despite pressure from the parents who were friends of a board member. This administrator said she would not give in because of the family's motivation for the move, which was to move the student into a less racially diverse school. She said: "Even though school board members are powerful and, I suspect, could get me fired, I would not compromise that position."

Another administrator expressed the opposite attitude, saying, "I don't want parents calling my area director complaining about the way I discipline students in my building, so I don't have trouble compromising discipline because discipline can get parents so upset." These two responses illustrate that administrators, through their personal characteristics, must choose where to make their stands with regard to the individual and situational pressures of organizational life. They also illustrate that compromise can serve as conflict avoidance.

Courage can also be a factor in ethical compromise and less-than-honest behavior. Lack of courage can come from a desire to avoid conflict. One participant said about his hiding of administrative travel money, "It is unethical that I hide it; I'm not brave enough to show it up front." Rather than frame the hiding of travel money as politically clever or necessary, this participant simply said he lacked the courage to not hide his travel funds. This is an example of a situation in which it may simply be too difficult for administrators to tell the whole truth.

Viewed from the individual perspective, the administrators' comments show that candor, compromise, and courage are personal characteristics they are sometimes able to draw upon in difficult situations. They might use them to regulate their own behavior, protect themselves, make their stands in terms of how much they'll give to the organization, or respond to situations in which it is simply much easier to leave some things left unsaid.

Personal Experiences

The participants said that the personal experiences of lying to protect staff and protecting personal and organizational priorities bothered their consciences. Some administrators, because of their personal experience, might lie to protect others. As one participant said, "If I could see a staff member was really vulnerable, I would lie to protect him instead of hurt him because I've been in a difficult situation, too."

Then there is the issue of keeping bad news in-house. It was common to hear these administrators speak of protecting their schools by keeping negative issues from reaching the central office, the school board, or the media. Another type of response regarding the protection of individual and organizational priorities had to do with school budgets. Administrators spoke about hiding funds to protect priorities that others don't buy into. One participant said, "I can be dishonest about certain views of the budget to protect my ability to put funds where I think they most need to be."

Personal Beliefs and Values

The administrators said that their beliefs and values about cultural differences and personal judgments could contribute to deception. The participants spoke of their experiences with cultural differences regarding the supervision of minority student teachers and the differential treatment of minority students.

One administrator, in discussing his discomfort regarding the ways he saw minority students being given allowances for negative behavior that nonminorities were not allowed, said he eventually realized that "that's the way life is, and there's not anything I can do about it so I might just as well accept it." He was somewhat anxious about his statement, saying, "I'm not sure if that's the way I want to be, and I'm not sure if that's not the way I want to be. I am more and more convinced that there is a real and obvious difference in cultures and that we have to make allowances." Another administrator expressed concern for black males in her district. She said, "The statistics for kids who are in special education are boys—black males. I don't want to put these kids there because the statistics bear out and say these kids tend to be that way."

These school administrators talked about how their personal judgments can make decision-making tougher and sometimes result in deception. A comment that illustrates the conflict inherent in an administrator's efforts to meet student needs serves as an example: "This business is one of looking at individual situations, but I suspect that 99% of the time I will always push for what, from my judgment, is in the best interest of the kid, and that sometimes will compromise what staff members consider to be responsibility on the part of the student." This person said she knows that some teachers on her staff view her student-centered efforts as putting them in ethically difficult positions.

A contrasting example of the problematic nature of personal judgments is one participant's discussion of why he hides funds and prints inaccurate copies of his budget. He said he relies on his "higher sense of order rather than trust that through a democracy we're all going to arrive at the same place at the same time."

Not all of these school administrators were comfortable with having their personal judgments play a large role in their decisions. As one said, "I think those are ways we get ourselves into real trouble when we just start ignoring things and saying we're going to do it a different way or we're going to get around it. If we're not following the guidelines or the policy, where are the kids going to be?"

The individual perspective reveals that administrators' personal characteristics, their experiences, and their beliefs and values are key components in the ways they find their way through the problem of deception as they deal with the pressures of organizational life. In negotiating the path between ethical compromise and deception, these administrators identified the types of less-than-honest behavior in which they might engage as:

1. Lying to protect others
2. Relying on candor to moderate the deception used to benefit themselves
3. Compromising to benefit others
4. Compromising to benefit themselves
5. Compromising to avoid conflict or making a stand
6. Holding back from telling the whole truth
7. Treating people differently

8. Not trusting the democratic process
9. Relying on their own judgment rather than preferences of others.

INTERPERSONAL THEORY AND FINDINGS

The interpersonal perspective or organizational analysis allows us to look at the ways in which group members interact. Doing so allows us to examine group dynamics with respect to improving the group's accomplishment of task functions, maintenance (process) functions, and other ways group members work together. For these administrators, less-than-honest behavior had to do with the organizational dynamics of (a) group norms, (b) sanctions, (c) conflict and conflict avoidance, and (d) in-group/out-group dynamics.

Group Norms

Communication, compromise, and building trust were the three components of group norms through which the administrators have experienced ethical quandaries and subsequent deception. One participant clearly identified the communication norm of indiscussability in his situation by pointing out that "there are times when it is too difficult to say what you think is going on." Another pointed out the relationship between the group norms of indiscussability and honest or dishonest behavior: "There is the real definition of honesty: how much can we say 'Here are all the facts—even the ones you didn't ask for—that could influence you'?"

A second group norm identified as troublesome is that of compromise, or accepting negative situations. One participant described his discomfort with prevailing attitudes and practices toward minority students. He said, "I came into an environment where that was happening and I accepted it and went on with it." This norm appears to be linked to indiscussability in that if there are times when it is too difficult to say what one thinks is going on, accepting it and moving on might be the only response the organizational norms will tolerate.

Another example of the group norm of compromise is the situation in which, despite state law, administrators are "led to believe that you had better have your ducks in order before you call Child Protective Services." The norm is: "Don't call Child Protective Services on suspicion, although it may be well-founded. You better have objective data." A participant summarized her concerns with this norm as a guide for behavior: "I think those are sometimes how we get ourselves into real trouble, when we start ignoring things. They result in compromises that are more extensive."

The third type of group norm identified as troublesome and leading, possibly, to less-than-honest behavior, is that of building trust among the staff. In describing her level of supervision regarding the reporting of extra hours by her staff, one participant said, "If they tell me these are the hours they work, I accept that and that is just to build trust." Another participant said that in his efforts to build trust among his staff and maintain his relationship with a teacher, he might "uphold a teacher's poor discipline and sacrifice the student."

Sanctions

Participants revealed that the interpersonal dynamic of sanctioning that takes place when group norms are broken has created ethically compromising situations for them. They reported feeling divided as a result of receiving the sanctions of (a) being warned against honesty and (b) experiencing negative relations with superiors.

Some administrators discussed situations in which, after sharing negative concerns with their superiors, they had been warned against being honest. For example: "You would be warned by your superior, 'That kind of information is not needed.'" Another administrator talked about a situation in which, although she carefully followed district procedure, her decision was reversed. "You see, they would have liked me to make an ethical compromise, but I followed the rule. Obviously, that wasn't their desire." As a result of not compromising her concern for her district's policy, she was subject to strained and chilly relations with a superior. This participant commented that it is a "strange conflict to be following the board policy and also supporting our program, only to find myself being criticized for a decision that was abiding by their policy."

A final example of sanctioning upon breaking a group norm is that of an administrator who shared his concern regarding the flight of district administrators to other districts. After expressing his concern at a district meeting, he was given unrealistically burdensome assignments, accompanied by none of the customary assistance or release time.

These examples illustrate the feelings of ethical compromise and the potential for subsequent less-than-honest behavior that can result from receiving sanctions for communicating bad news, following district procedure, and expressing concerns for organizational stability and loyalty. Some administrators report that they have ceased communicating bad news to the central office and now keep conflict and compromise in-house. Others report they are more likely to discern a superior's desire, rather than follow district policy, when making a decision. Viewing these responses from the interpersonal perspective illustrates the manner in which the organizational dynamic of sanctioning, which typically takes place after group norms are broken, can lead to less-than-honest behavior on the part of well-intentioned district administrators.

Conflict

Participants' responses reveal that the group dynamics associated with conflict and its avoidance has resulted in ethically troublesome workplace behaviors. Conflict and its avoidance appear to be associated with fears of parental reaction and fears of in-group/out-group dynamics.

One participant made the first fear explicit, saying, "I've been guilty of not notifying parents of student behaviors because we're afraid of parental reaction." Another explained, "We sometimes allow things to happen because we don't really want to call up the parents and tell them we think their kid's a little crazy." The consequences of the fear of parental reaction can have far-reaching effects. One person admitted, "We don't want to upset parents, so we are sometimes hesitant to call Child Protective Services."

Finally, an issue associated with conflict and its avoidance is that of in-group/out-group dynamics. The manner in which participants discussed this issue typically included the protection of resources and private agendas. For example, one participant discussed the issue this way: "There are some circumstances where deceptive behavior is justified. The budget is one of them. Site-based management and decision-making is another. Who ought to be part of being in the know and who ought to just know afterwards what the result is?"

Applying the interpersonal perspective to the principals' comments reveals that as administrators encounter situations created by the organizational dynamics of group norms, sanctions, conflict and conflict avoidance, and in-group/out-group dynamics, they are likely to experience some sense of ethical compromise.

The types of less-than-honest behavior shown to result from these organizational dynamics include:

1. Hiding bad news
2. Accepting situations perceived as negative
3. Disregarding public laws
4. Disregarding supervisory responsibilities
5. Disregarding students' rights
6. Failing to inform parents of student issues
7. Excluding others from public process, and ignoring district policy and procedure.

CULTURAL THEORY AND FINDINGS

Where the interpersonal perspective provides insight into the day-to-day interactions among group members and how they evolve into group dynamics, the cultural perspective helps us understand how those dynamics evolve into common understandings and norms of behavior among group members. Thus, the cultural perspective looks for common understandings in groups. The relevant situations had to do with (a) values, (b) organizational norms, (c) organizational sanctions,

(d) socialization, (e) cultural diversity, and (f) miscellaneous other topics.

Values

The values identified through this perspective had to do with concern for the welfare of students. One participant said, "We can't be giving double messages: Either we care or we don't." The stance of the participants, expressed in a variety of ways, was, "We are here to help your kids; we may have to break the rules to do so."

Organizational Norms

Five behaviors emerge as the most troublesome of the organizational norms the participants experienced in learning and carrying out their roles as school administrators. The participants report they learned to, or saw others:

1. Misrepresent themselves
2. Accept ethically compromising situations
3. Acknowledge that honesty is not an option
4. Trade silence for safety, avoid conflict
5. Treat some rules differentially.

When their responses regarding these norms of behavior are arranged in order, from the administrator with the least experience to the administrator with the most experience, the norms appear to describe a progressive order, from consciously looking for the norms of the role to matter-of-factly creating alternate ways of meeting children's needs and ignoring rules to meet the needs of individuals. In other words, as time goes on, principals resign themselves to working the angles to benefit the kids.

For example, in finally getting her first job of principal, the most recently hired participant consciously looked for ways to appear to fit the role of principal. She says, "For years I was looking for the mold to get the position. I think I did misrepresent myself to get the job."

The administrator next in order of experience spoke of learning that "in some situations, I finally realized that that's the way life is, and there's not anything I can do about it, so I might as well accept it." He says his suspicions were reinforced upon consulting his superior. "I was honest with my boss about my perceptions and she said, 'Yeah, that's the way things are.'"

Third, in learning the norms required to be seen as successful and to keep the position, one administrator said, "Honesty is not an option. You have to report that everything is okay and give as little negative information as possible." In talking about not getting a job because of an affirmative-action hire, another participant agreed that honesty is not an option. She said, "I am not sure I could think of anything to do differently except that I would have preferred that the interview committee would have been honest with me, and that is simply not an option."

One participant said that the organizational pressure to be silent about bad news in exchange for positional safety could lead to less-than-honest behavior. "An example is the test scores last year. Rather than deal with the problem, we hear 'You will raise test scores, period.' That's the kind of environment that fosters deception in order to raise test scores."

Another of the participants, in recalling his previous boss, said, "I saw how he would tiptoe around union and discipline issues. That is how he and other administrators are successful." Another participant reported how important it is for him to avoid conflict in dealing with certain minority children: "I find myself being very cautious. I let minority students see what I'm writing in my documentation."

Finally, with regard to rules, descriptions from those administrators with the most experience reveal a sense of autonomy and professional judgment not present in the earlier statements. One person said, "It sounds like we're running a real dishonest operation here, but I think there are lots of occurrences where, for the welfare of the kids, and the care of the kids, we choose to find some alternate ways of operating." Another said: "None of us fit in boxes. And so I do participate in deceptive behavior because you have to meet the needs of the individual, and laws are made for groups."

Organizational Sanctions

In the dynamic of organizational sanctions, two issues were revealed. They were intolerant superintendents sanctioning the communication of bad news, and the threat of legal action sanctioning the communication of honest information. The participants reported that these sanctions left them feeling ethically conflicted. One person said, "We didn't want things to go downtown because our superintendent was not very tolerant." Another was told not to share bad news with district officials. Asked what would happen if he did, he said, "Your competency would be questioned; you would be humiliated in a public meeting."

The threat of legal action was another sanction mentioned. In discussing the issue of affirmative action versus hiring based on merit, one person said, "The world being as it is, if they are totally honest with me then they put themselves in a point of liability." Such a sanction limits honest communication and, in effect, creates a situation in which organizational members are pressured to be evasive, to be strategically ambiguous, or to tell outright lies.

Socialization

The participants have clearly been exposed to some degree of socialization regarding using ambiguous language to hide their intentions and treating people differently because of race. With regard to the first of the two, one participant said principals do not have a say in who transfers into their buildings. To deal with that, a mentor taught her to describe the position in such a way as to discourage unwanted transferees. For example: "If I'm looking for someone to be coaching, coaching what? A teacher? Students? Computer class?" Being strategically vague helps this administrator shape her staff to her needs.

With regard to differential treatment based on race, a participant said he was mentored in a way that made him feel uncomfortable. He said that after it was obvious to him that minority students were treated more leniently about their behavior than other students, he discussed the issue with his boss. This person said that as a result of that conversation, he has learned, "We *do* accept behavior from minorities that we would not accept from other kids. In order to keep minority kids in school, you have to make allowances, and the allowances can' t be that you have increased their reading scores, so you have to allow minorities more latitude in the way they conduct themselves." This issue was also raised by the person who said, "I know of a teacher of color who is not doing well. People are bending over backwards to fix it, and it's not working. Are we bending over backwards more because of color, or would we do it for anyone?"

Cultural Diversity

The element of cultural diversity appears from the cultural perspective as an organizational dynamic that has caused the participants some degree of ethical compromise. The interview responses fell into two categories: ethnicity as a part of self, and cultural diversity at school.

In discussing ethnicity and cultural diversity, one participant said, "My ethnicity is part of who I am. I was raised in an area where I didn't only see white people. My cousins are people of color. I just didn't get the dark skin. And I never thought it made a difference, but it does." Another person said that being "the only child who had the coloring I have made me realize all the discrimination of being poor, of being a different color." Coming from families of color has made a difference in their outlooks concerning the issue of cultural diversity in schools.

An example of this difference can be seen in the way some of the administrators view their work with regard to issues of cultural diversity. One apparently Caucasian administrator, who made no mention of any ethnic or cultural diversity in his background, also made no mention of student needs with regard to cultural diversity in his school. A second apparently Caucasian administrator, who also made no mention of any ethnic or cultural diversity in his background, described "making allowances for minorities, and the allowance can't be that you have increased their reading scores, so you have to allow minority kids more latitude in the way they conduct themselves."

In contrast to the above, a third apparently Caucasian administrator said her thinking about cultural diversity had changed as a result of not getting a position due to an affirmative-action hire. This person said experiencing that situation "made me more sensitive to minority viewpoints. I had never walked in those shoes before. I had always been part of the majority, the group influencing the decision. This gave me a chance to feel what other folks have felt."

The two administrators who discussed the importance of their ethnicity were also the only ones who spoke of the importance of school as a place for raising children's sensitivities to cultural diversity. Both pointed out the importance of minority hires, and one suggested that this was a good way to heighten cultural awareness. This same person said he felt compromised by a superior's revision of the school's Christmas program. "I wanted our programs to be diverse, not empty of meaning. As a result of this compromise, we ended up doing Frosty the Snowman stuff."

Finally, with regard to increasing diversity in schools, one person spoke of her district's hiring efforts. She said, "In our district, a couple of administrators interviewed a lot of people of color so that they could be immediately hired. Then other administrators said, 'If I can't find anyone else, then I'll take from that pool.'"

Miscellaneous

Status, rituals, and conflict avoidance, although reported less frequently than the issues cited in the previous sections, play a role in ethical compromise. In regard to status, one principal said, "I would not confront a board member because that's not my place." Referring to his concern for a culturally rich and diverse Christmas program being overruled by a supervisor who wanted the program to be culture-free, this person said, "The ritual of the Christmas program was thus emptied of meaning, as are other rituals. We're constantly on the mark to do public relations things like Grandparents' Day, but the real purpose is to get voters into the school to see how wonderful we are. When rituals are enacted for ulterior motives, they lose their potency."

Finally, conflict avoidance was examined from the cultural perspective. As in the interpersonal analysis section, conflict avoidance appears to be associated with fearfulness regarding how parents will react.

The cultural perspective, then, shows us that as school administrators encountered situations created by the organizational dynamics of values, prevailing norms, organizational sanctions, socialization, and cultural diversity, they felt some sense of ethical compromise and expressed concern over the resulting less-than-honest behavior. The types of less-than-honest behavior following from these organizational dynamics include:

1. Misrepresenting themselves
2. Accepting negative situations
3. Hiding bad news
4. Disregarding public laws
5. Using strategic ambiguity
6. Treating people differently based on race.

POLITICAL THEORY AND FINDINGS

Promoting one's own interests is the primary dynamic of political behavior. The political perspective maintains that groups, their differences, and the struggle for resources will always lead to political conflict. Thus, the political perspective views organizations as environments in which individuals and coalitions use power to control resources, manipulate communication, and influence others to get what they want. From the political perspective, the situations and dynamics behind these administrators' ethical compromise had to do with (a) interests, (b) use of power, (c) resources, (d) coalitions, and (e) conflict. In some instances, power and interests were seen to be merged in the form of coalitions. Each of these areas will be discussed separately.

Interests

According to these school administrators, personal interests can be a source of ethical compromise in that individuals might feel compelled to engage in less-than-honest behaviors in order to promote their own interests or to protect their interests. For example, one participant reported hearing of a principal's being asked by a superior to "change their recommendation for an intern to make it sound better." Another participant reported that, in order to improve his chances for advancement, he learned to not share negative news with central office. This person said the same approach applies to his communication with parents. "We certainly want to play down violence. Perception is everything. My goal is to have parents believe I manage a safe environment where it probably is not always safe. I think I am more guilty of that than anything else."

Participants reported that they protected their interests by acting deceptively in the following ways: (a) jockeying for position, (b) manipulating information, (c) hiding funds, (d) lying for what is right, and (e) protecting one's self.

Jockeying for Position

Two of the participants described situations in which they engaged in less-than-honest behavior in the attempt to gain or increase their positional power. One person said, "I think I did [represent myself differently] than who I am to get something I want. For years I was looking for 'Where's the mold to get this position, what's the game, where are the hoops?'"

Manipulating Information

Another person said, "Certainly in education we all want to look as good as possible. We might withhold or give out information, sometimes at the expense of somebody else, because it will make them look good or enhance their career, or because we want to look as good as possible."

Hiding Funds

Throughout the interviews, the issue of funds as scarce resources showed up as an organizational dynamic behind less-than-honest behavior. From the political perspective of promoting and protecting interests, one participant said he feels compelled to hide funds because "As we move toward democratic process in setting priorities and involving others in decisions, we have to act on a higher sense of order, rather than trust that through a democracy we're all going to arrive at the same place at the same time."

Lying for What Is Right

One participant's comments had specifically to do with lying: "There are times we can't tell the whole truth about everything we know because there's a greater good to be accomplished." He added, "There are some circumstances where deceptive behavior is justified. Budget is one of them. Site-based management and decision-making is another." This participant concluded, "There's a difference between lying for what's right and lying for what's wrong."

Protecting One's Self

In describing how he might be forced to protect himself from his superintendent's efforts to pressure him out of his position, one participant said, "I'm not going to let him jeopardize my financial position. I'm not going to let him jeopardize my family. I don't need to participate in a lot of the things that make him look good. That's probably what I'll do, is withdraw from things that make him look good." From a political perspective, such behavior can be described as withholding expert power as a means of self-protection.

Use of Power

Participants described feelings of compromise as a result of being subjected to coercive power. Such situations are (a) top-down demands, (b) a board member exerting pressure to receive special treatment, counter to district policy, and (c) being forced to undertake a building remodel, without assistance, as a perceived consequence for speaking out.

Top-Down Demands

One of the participants said, "If our last superintendent was [sic] here, I think I'd be running more scared right now because of all the hidden agendas. Because of the top-down, because of the 'You don't say, you don't breathe, you'd better look this way.'" Another person said he was told, "All news has to be good news. No matter how things are going, report that everything is okay." In addition, this participant said his superior warned him that certain kinds of information were not needed. This person was told that his "chances for advancement would be simpler" if he followed these suggestions.

Exerting Pressure to Receive Preferential Treatment

Another example of the use of coercive power leading to feelings of ethical compromise is this description. After she turned down a request by a parent in her school (who happened to be a district board member) to allow that parent's child to attend a school outside of the attendance area, that board member sought, and received, a different decision from the principal's superior. The principal said, "I find myself feeling criticized by who is eventually my boss, the school board, for a decision that was abiding by their policy. That makes me a little uncomfortable. I wonder where I'm going to work next year, you know?"

Consequence for Speaking Out

A final example of the use of coercive power is the situation in which a principal was forced to undertake the remodeling of his building, without being granted any release time or a project manager, as a consequence for speaking out about school district loyalty. This person said, "Almost everyone in the curriculum department left last year: the superintendent was a finalist in another job; the assistant superintendent took a job as superintendent in another district; the elementary director took a job as assistant superintendent in another district; the secondary director was interviewing. I asked, 'What happened to loyalty? Why aren't our children as good to work for as children in other districts? Is positional power that important that we forget our mission?' I said that in a public meeting, so I think that's what happened to me." This situation also serves as example of the "all news has to be good news" rule described earlier.

Resources

As described earlier, the allocation of resources can be used to sanction the behavior of others. From a political perspective, the use of funds in this manner can be defended by a superior simply stating that the issue really is a money issue. One participant wondered, "Is it really a money issue or is there a subtext? I don't know . . ." From the political perspective, the allocation of funds, regardless of motive, can be seen as a source of conflict.

Other administrators spoke of the conflict they face with the administrative travel portion of their school budget. They report feeling compelled to hide the money allotted for their in-district travel expenses because "You have to come to grips with why the principal is taking $200 out of the building budget when paper is needed. The politics get involved."

Coalitions

In some instances, power and interests were seen to be merged in the form of coalitions. Coalitions can be another form of self-protection. One participant described the conflict he faces in "trying to uphold the discipline of a teacher that you truly do not believe was good discipline, and you uphold what the teacher wants for the sake of a relationship. You can't win every battle, and you really feel that you are sacrificing the kid." The principal's upholding of a teacher's poor discipline for the "sake of a relationship" can be viewed as a coalition.

Conflict

The primary sources of conflict, from a political perspective, were the allocation of scarce resources and dealing with coalitions, both of which were discussed earlier. The typical responses to these situations were to exclude others from decision-making processes, hide information, hide funds, and compromise other people.

Politically speaking, as administrators encountered situations created by the organizational dynamics of interests, power, resources, coalitions, and conflict, they felt some sense of ethical compromise and expressed concern for resultant less-than-honest behavior. The types of less-than-honest behavior shown to result from these organizational dynamics include:

1. Altering letters of recommendation
2. Hiding bad news
3. Misrepresenting self
4. Manipulating information
5. Hiding funds
6. Lying for what is considered right.

SUMMARY

School administrators interact daily with students, teachers, support staff, parents, other administrators, and central office personnel, all of whom look for and expect to find resolutions to their problems from them. The analysis of the interviews from the structural, individual, interpersonal, cultural, and political perspectives of organizational theory shows that school administrators are not necessarily able to meet all the needs of each of these groups. An organizational analysis reveals the many ways school administrators are faced with complex situations in which less-than-honest behavior may be the only way they can see to manage the conflicting demands of all the populations they serve.

The interviews reveal the types of pressures placed on school administrators and describe the types of less-than-honest behavior in which they engage as a result of the pressures brought to bear by the organization.

The structural perspective showed that roles, resources, and rules can and do result in ethically compromising situations for administrators with respect to maintaining productivity, protecting children, influencing decisions, and protecting resources.

From the individual perspective, the pressures were identified to be personal characteristics and experiences, personal beliefs and values, cultural differences, and the characteristics of others.

From the interpersonal perspective, the pressures of group norms, sanctions, and conflict were found to result in less-than-honest behavior.

From the cultural perspective, relevant pressures were values, problematic organizational norms, organizational sanctions, some types of socialization, and issues of cultural diversity.

Finally, from the political perspective, the organizational pressures school administrators face emerged from interests, power, resources, coalitions, and conflict.

The results of these organizational dynamics placed participants in situations in which they reported behaving deceptively. From a structural perspective, participants reported that they or others forged documentation or results, bent or ignored rules, hid funds, manipulated procedures, ignored policy, and gave out partial or misleading information.

Individual dynamics led them to lie in order to protect others, to compromise to benefit others and avoid conflict, to treat people unequally, and to rely on their own judgment. Less-than-honest behaviors associated with the interpersonal dynamics of organizational life included hiding bad news, accepting negative situations, disregarding public laws, disregarding supervisory responsibilities, disregarding student rights, failing to give parents relevant information, excluding others from public process, and ignoring district policy and procedure.

As a result of cultural dynamics, participants admitted that they had misrepresented themselves, accepted negative situations, hid bad news, disregarded public laws, engaged in strategic ambiguity, and treated people differently because of race.

Finally, the types of dishonest behavior participants reported as resulting from the political dynamics of organizational life included altering letters of recommendation, keeping bad news hidden from both central office and parents, misrepresenting themselves, manipulating information, hiding funds, and lying for what they considered right. The most common of these behaviors were hiding bad news, hiding money, and treating people in similar situations differently.

Through their candid examination of their own professional practice, these brave people have helped solidify the understanding that the onus of less-than-honest behavior rests not only on the individual, but also that powerful organizational pressures do come into play. When all news has to be good news, when resources are inadequate to support district initiatives, or when district initiatives fail to take cultural realities into account, the experiences of this group show that organizational dynamics can result in less-than-honest behavior.

6

Interpersonal Dynamics

All men should strive to learn before they die what they are running from, and to, and why.

—James Thurber

What is the human dimension of less-than-honest behavior in organizational life? In attempting to answer this question, I looked at the interview data from six perspectives of social psychology. As presented in chapter 3, they are learning theory, cognitive theory, motivation theory, decision-making theory, social exchange theory, and role theory.

Each of these theories emphasizes one aspect of the causes of deceptive behavior without necessarily claiming that the others are unimportant or irrelevant. Some similar threads run through the different perspectives. For example, cognitive theory and motivation theory are akin in their perception of the individual. Cognitive theory contends that current perceptions are the key factors in the decision to engage in less-than-honest behavior. Motivation theory contends that social situations can create individuals' needs, and that those needs influence perceptions and behavior.

Learning Theory and Findings

According to learning theory, deceptive behavior is shaped by past learning. In any given situation, a person learns certain behaviors that may become habits. People learn through association, reinforcement, observational learning, and imitation or modeling. Learning theory contends that behavior results from previous learning, not from psy-

103

chological or subjective states. Through this lens, the interviewees' less-than-honest behavior was seen as having been shaped by (a) common practice, (b) experience, and (c) mentoring.

Common Practice

Six types of less-than-honest behavior were identified as common practice. The administrators reported witnessing, experiencing, or learning to: hide bad news, use less-than-honest behaviors to create high test scores, provide extra overload time to staff, claim partial days as full days, treat minorities differently than nonminorities, and compromise discipline and policy to avoid conflict with superiors and parents.

Experience

Five types of less-than-honest behavior were identified as having been learned through individual experience. Those behaviors were lying to protect others, failing to intervene on students' behalf to avoid conflict with teachers, being dishonest with regard to affirmative action hires, being dishonest to protect the organization, and hiding funds to protect them.

Mentoring

The administrators reported having learned three types of less-than-honest behavior through mentoring. Those behaviors were using strategic ambiguity, adhering to different standards with minorities than with whites, and compromising to avoid conflict.

Cognitive Theory

Cognitive theory posits that our behavior depends on our social perceptions. Thus, deceptive behavior is affected by individual characteristics, such as personality and ability, and by the social environment as it is perceived. Cognitive theorists examine deception as a product of current perceptions rather than as a product of past learning. They look at how people integrate information to arrive at conclusions about the social world, and at how they act deceptively as a result. Through this perspective, less-than-honest behavior on the part of these five administrators was seen as having been created as a result of (a) the social environment, (b) individual perceptions, and (c) individual personalities.

Social Environment

Seen through this lens, the principals engaged in six types of less-than-honest behavior created by the social environment. Those behaviors were using nondisclosure to protect themselves and others, hiding bad news, creating false images about school safety, accepting negative situations, using different standards with regard to minority students' academic performance and physical behavior, and hiding funds to avoid conflict.

Individual Perceptions

Individual perceptions contributed to five types of less-than-honest behavior. Those behaviors were compromising to meet students' needs, treating students differently to protect them, using different standards when hiring minorities to benefit students, hiding funds, and withholding information to achieve their own sense of a greater good.

Individual Personalities

Four types of less-than-honest behavior were attributed to individual personalities. Participants say they ignored or broke rules to protect students, broke rules on discipline to avoid conflict with parents, broke rules to meet others' needs, and strayed from the truth to protect others and to avoid conflict.

Motivation Theory and Findings

According to motivation theorists, people deceive to satisfy a need or a desire. Social psychologists examine ways in which specific situations and relationships can create motives. These administrators' responses indicated that their less-than-honest behavior came out of their individual needs to (a) protect, (b) avoid conflict, and (c) carry out their individual sense of the greater good.

Protect

Participants said they felt the need to deceive staff to protect themselves and their time, to hide bad news to protect their images and careers, and to withhold information from others to look good. They were less-than-honest about their level of supervision to protect their staff, lied to protect others, undermined teachers to protect students, hid the truth to protect teachers and colleagues, and bent rules to meet the needs of students, teachers, and colleagues. The administrators also lied to protect the resource of time, and lied about the budget and hid funds in order to protect fiscal resources. Finally, they reported being evasive to protect the organization.

Avoid Conflict

In their attempts to keep the peace, the interviewees chose not to enforce student discipline, hid funds, and were less than strict about complying with child protection laws. Their intent was to avoid conflict with parents, teachers, students, and interest groups.

Carry Out Individual Sense of Greater Good

Attempting to achieve what they considered to be a greater good, the participants used three forms of deception. They used different standards when hiring minorities to ensure that students would have a broader experience; they ignored or bent state law to help students earn specific credits; and they ignored democratic process and hid funds to achieve specific priorities.

Decision-Making Theory and Findings

According to decision-making theories, people figure out the likely outcomes of various actions and pick the best alternatives in a fairly logical and reasoned way. In other words, their lies are planned. Lies are simply seen as viable options in particular situations. In this study, lying was seen as the best alternative to:

1. Protect
2. Avoid conflict
3. Carry out the administrators' own sense of greater good.

Because these findings are similar to the less-than-honest behaviors identified through motivation theory, minor differences will be pointed out.

Protect

The participants reported deceiving to protect others, the organization, resources, and self, in that order. From a motivation perspective, protecting self was the primary motive; from a decision-making perspective, protecting self was reported least often.

The types of less-than-honest behavior in which participants said they engaged to protect others were: lying, circumventing policies to protect teachers' aide time, using different standards to protect minority students, bending policy and procedure to serve student needs, withholding information about credits to protect students who might be unable to use the information, and using deception to meet the human needs of individuals. The types of less-than-honest behavior participants used to protect the organization were teaching to the test to show improved test scores, playing down violence to create a false image of school safety, and withholding public information from students about credits in order to protect the organization from its inability to meet student requests.

The one type of less-than-honest behavior in which participants said they decided to engage to protect resources was hiding funds in the school budget. To protect themselves, however, the principals hid bad news, were strategically ambiguous, compromised their own values, and withdrew from specific activities to avoid making a superior look good.

Avoid Conflict

To avoid conflict, the administrators accepted negative situations, went easy on misbehaving students, and hid funds. They also did one thing not noted through the motivation perspective: they hid bad news to avoid conflict with the superintendent.

Carry Out Own Sense of Greater Good

To achieve what they considered to be a greater good, participants engaged in four less-than-honest behaviors. They compromised policy and procedure with regard to reimbursing the general fund, hid certain facts, excluded people from the democratic process, and hid funds to further specific goals.

Social Exchange Theory and Findings

Social exchange theorists do not focus on the behavior of the individual but rather on the behaviors of two or more individuals who interact with each other. In social exchange theory, as two people interact with each other, they exchange benefits and costs. With regard to less-than-honest behavior, social exchange theory analyzes interaction between individuals on the basis of costs and benefits to each. This study showed that less-than-honest behavior was seen as part of the process of benefiting (a) self, (b) students, and (c) staff. Only one example was given of the potential costs of interpersonal interactions.

Self

Because student test scores are a factor in the evaluation of administrators, falsely creating high test scores was seen as a self-benefiting behavior. Because giving ambiguous or misleading information to a potential transfer teacher might dissuade that teacher from making the move, that behavior, too, was seen as self-benefiting. Working a few hours a day and counting it as a full day was seen as financially self-benefiting. Finally, avoiding conflict and hiding bad news were identified as self-benefiting behaviors because they make the administrators look competent.

Students

A school's treatment team decision to ignore district policy and procedure to serve a student was seen, through the perspective of cognitive theory, as benefiting students. An administrator's urging a teacher to operate outside of the norm regarding grading practices was perceived as benefiting students. Ignoring accounting guidelines to buy washing machines and hot lunches for students was considered beneficial for them.

Staff

Staff was seen as benefiting from three behaviors: bending policy and procedure to provide continued aide time for teachers, supporting teachers who use poor discipline, and ignoring district policy to provide release time for teachers.

Role Theory and Findings

Role theorists examine group norms concerning roles and the ways in which individuals adapt their roles to better fit their goals and needs. Less-than-honest behavior on the part of these five administrators could be a result of either following preexisting scripts in the role of administrator, or creating individual scripts in the role of administrator. Through this perspective, less-than-honest behavior was seen as a result of (a) administrators following group norms in the role of administrator, or (b) administrators creating individual adaptations to the role of school administrator.

Group Norms

The less-than-honest behavior participants identified as a result of group norms concerning the administrator's role were: ignoring district policy and procedure to provide extra aide time for teachers; hiding bad news; ignoring the real problems with standardized test scores and then "gaming the system" to improve test scores; treating minority students differently with regard to behavior and academic performance; easing up on discipline to avoid conflict; realizing that for an organizational representative, honesty is not an option in some situations; realizing that breaking rules is necessary in some cases to care for people; and ignoring the law to protect the home/school relationship.

Individual Adaptations

As a result of their own individual adaptations to the administrator's role, the participants practiced six less-than-honest behaviors. These behaviors were ignoring district policy and procedure to avoid labeling a child as behaviorally disturbed, changing a grade a teacher had given to benefit a student, ignoring democratic process to protect funds and priorities, ignoring school district accounting procedures in order to protect school funds and benefit students, treating students differently with regard to testing, and compromising district rules to meet the needs of others.

In order to meet the needs of their various constituents and achieve the many conflicting goals of their middle-management positions, the principals interviewed have either followed existing group norms concerning principals or have adapted their roles individually. The less-than-honest behaviors described above were the result. The perspective of role theory reveals the types of less-than-honest behavior that result from principals' individual adaptations to their roles, or from group norms regarding the role of administrator.

In order to meet the needs of their various constituents and to achieve the many conflicting goals and priorities of their positions, these principals have either developed individual adaptations to, or have followed existing group norms of, the role of administrator.

In order to meet the needs of others, the participants reported ignoring district policy and procedure, compromising rules and laws, and compromising other people. In order to achieve specific district priorities, the participants reported ignoring democratic process, hiding bad news, ignoring problems and procedures with standardized test scores, and practicing differentiated treatment. All of the participants admitted that in some situations honesty is not an option.

SUMMARY

One of the purposes of this book is to draw upon the integrative aspects of social psychology to explore how personal and interpersonal dynamics might shape responses to ethically difficult situations on the part of school administrators. This analysis from the six major perspectives of social psychology theory shows that individuals don't operate out of any single set of driving principles. Rather, individuals operate from driving forces that can best be understood from a variety of perspectives.

The categories of less-than-honest behaviors most widely represented across all six perspectives of the analysis of the data through social psychology theory are, in order of frequency: compromising policies, procedures, rules, or laws; hiding bad news; using nondisclosure or strategic ambiguity; hiding funds; engaging in differential treatment.

A major contribution of the findings from these interviews is its evidence of the humanity of school leaders. In contrast to the myth of the heroic leader who faces crises without flinching, makes difficult decisions without ethical compromise, and blithely implements organizational initiatives without blinking twice, the tales these courageous people tell describe the imperfect world of school organizations as navigated by flesh-and-blood human beings who engage in deceptive behavior from time to time. Rather than using such evidence to condemn individuals, this work is part of a growing body of leadership literature that recognizes the conflicts inherent in the administrative role.

7

Professional Ethics

An unjust law is itself a species of violence. Arrest for its breach is more so.

—Mohandas K. Gandhi

One purpose of this book about school administrators balancing a complex array of dynamics to achieve the greater good is to understand how these administrators might approach and manage ethical decision-making. In this vein, this chapter presents the analysis of the interview responses from the five theoretical perspectives of ethical decision-making explored in chapter 4.

First, a brief restatement of the essential characteristics of each of these theoretical approaches.

Platonic theory ascribes to idealism and justice and is built upon rational laws that describe the parameters of justice. Chief among Plato's parameters of justice is *right action* toward all. Plato's theory holds that because leaders are responsible for the welfare of the people, leaders are obligated to show a high regard for due process of the law.

Hume disagreed with Plato's concept of justice as an outcome of rational laws. Instead, Hume believed that justice is simply that which proves to be most beneficial to society. He believed self-interest is natural, but that it should not occur at another's expense. Hume believed that justice and virtue are whatever society collectively determines, and, contrary to Plato, that any obligation to follow the law is based on nothing but the collective sentiments and interests of society.

Kantian theory is grounded in the power of reason, not Hume's sentiment, to guide decision-making. Kant formulated the categorical imperative as the way to judge the ethicality of an action. The categorical imperative asks: "Would it be good if my action became law, universally applicable to everybody?"

Mill's theory of ethics holds that *justice* is comprised of social utility, or the greatest benefit to the greatest number. Mill believed the goal of an action is the most important thing to consider, and that we are obligated to pursue the means that deliver the greatest good to the greatest number of people. Mill's utilitarianism contends that people should be free to do as they wish, as long as their actions do not hurt other people, and that leaders should use their skills to achieve the greatest good for the most people.

Downie and Telfer's ethics are based on respect for individuals. Their theory blends the concern for an ideal concept of justice with the use of reason and emotion, and holds that a basic respect for individuals is the key to what is ethical and just. Downie and Telfer's theory is one of absolute respect for people, yet it maintains that duty to self is not subordinated by duty to others.

Of course, none of these theorists spoke directly about the dilemmas school administrators face. Although school administrators' decision-making can be analyzed according to these five theories of ethics, administrators use a variety of ethical theories to make difficult decisions; it is not realistic to expect a patterned response to especially difficult situations.

SUMMARY OF FINDINGS

Ethical Theory

Following one's own sense of ethics can result in choosing behavior that is less-than-honest. Through this analysis, the administrators' less-than-honest behavior can be seen to have been shaped primarily by their concerns with doing what they consider to be humane for others, protecting children or meeting their needs, and, reported less frequently, protecting funds, the organization, and options.

Plato's Theory

Two responses were made with regard to a Platonic sense of due process of the law. One participant's response—"That's where my own value system is so strong in terms of being honest and following the rule as it is, and then working to change it if I don't believe in it"—led to another Platonic response: "Does following the rules put some kids in this school at a disadvantage? I won't do less, I can't do less. There have to be rules for conduct."

Even with these comments as background, this participant acknowledged the practice of "bending the rules" regarding credits for gym classes "because I consider it the humane thing to do." This same person also acknowledged the necessity of withholding information regarding the issue of variances with physical education credits to protect some students and to protect the organization: "If I think giving information about credits would harm kids because of their inability to use it, or because we don't have a process in line, then I would not give them the information." This participant articulated the Platonic ideals of justice and a high regard for the due process of law.

With regard to actual practice, this participant articulated two other ethical approaches: Mill's utilitarianism of using the skills of leadership to achieve the greatest good for the most people, and Downie and Telfer's respect for individuals.

Hume's Theory

Hume's approach to ethical decision-making asserts that justice is simply that which proves to be most beneficial to society and that any obligation to follow the law is based on interests and sentiments—as long as others are not hurt. Comments from one participant associated with Hume's approach have to do with "not saying anything negative because of better chances for advancement," "playing down violence because my goal is to have parents believe I manage a safe environment," "making allowances to keep minority kids in school," and "compromising discipline because discipline can get parents so upset." From another participant, the statement, "There's a difference between lying for what's right and lying for what's wrong," can be seen as being more closely related to Hume's approach than to any of the others.

Kant's Theory

None of the participants gave responses that appeared to come out of Kant's categorical imperative, which asks, "Would it be good if my action became a universal law applicable to everyone?" All the interviewees spoke about the ethically compromising situations they face and the conflicts that result. All of them described the less-than-honest behavior they used to resolve the conflicts. As mentioned earlier, one participant said, "I bend the rule because I consider it the humane and compassionate thing to do," but did not advise that as a course of action for everybody. Rather, this participant stated, "There have to be rules for conduct," and that it is important to "follow the rules." These responses are as close as any of the responses got to the Kantian examination of actions for the law of universal applicability.

Mill's Theory

Mill's theory of ethics, which holds that justice is a result of the greatest benefit for the most people and that leaders should use their skills to achieve that result, was one of the two significant ethical bases from which the five participants appear to operate. Nine responses were directly associated with Mill's utilitarianism. Among those is one discussed earlier, withholding information about PE credits. This participant said, "The area that you could say 'Here is an example of deceptive behavior occurring' might be in that situation where you don't necessarily offer up all of the information that you may know, like with PE. There is no way we could, as things are now, accommodate all the possibilities." In this case, withholding information was seen as the most effective way to protect the most people.

The other eight responses associated solely with Mill's utilitarianism came from one participant. The less-than-honest behaviors this person described were carried out to protect money rather than have it diverted to special interests, to meet children's needs rather than lose control of resources or options, and to increase the chances of achieving goals perceived to benefit the greater good.

Downie and Telfer's Theory

Downie and Telfer's theory of ethics was the other significant ethical base from which the five participants appear to operate. Responses clearly associated with Downie and Telfer's respect for individuals came from three of the participants. One of them made five comments directly related to respect for individuals, and the other two made one each. One of the singular responses was, "So I do participate in deceptive behavior because you have to meet the needs of the individual, and laws are made for groups." The other singular response is the already discussed statement, "I bend the rule (for a student's request regarding PE credits) because I consider it the humane and compassionate thing to do."

The other five responses associated solely with Downie and Telfer's respect for individuals came from one participant. The less-than-honest behaviors this person described were intended to protect individual children from being labeled or underserved by district programs, to protect members of a family from grief, and to protect staff members who might be vulnerable.

SUMMARY

Looking at the interview responses through the five perspectives of ethical theory shows that the participants drew primarily upon the theoretical principles of justice as described in Mill's theory of utilitarian ethics and in Downie and Telfer's theory based on respect for individuals. Kant's law of universal applicability didn't appear at all, and Plato's description of justice, in the case of one participant, served as a guide for ideals, not necessarily as a guide for practice.

Finally, several less-than-honest behaviors were used to resolve the ethical difficulties school administrators face. All five expressed the need to withhold information or to lie in order to protect other people and the organization. They all feel compelled to ignore, bend, or break policies, rules, and laws to meet the needs of children. Some of them said that they needed to practice differential treatment either to protect children or to meet their needs.

For these five school administrators, an ethical stance involved protecting values of justice and respect, usually with students at the center. In sincere responses to candid questions, these individuals described why they chose to ignore, bend, or break rules; why they chose not to disclose factual information; or why they lied. One after another, they admitted to deceiving others for many reasons, including self-protection, but usually in order to promote justice and compassion within the schools for which they were responsible.

The conclusions that can be drawn from the viewpoints of organizational theory, social psychology, and ethical decision-making as they apply to organizational dynamics and less-than-honest behavior are the subject of the next, and final, chapter.

Balancing It All

Justice is truth in action. Justice is the right of the weak.

—Joseph Joubert

Ethics and the School Administrator: Balancing Today's Complex Issues explores how school administrators might use less-than-honest behavior in working through the complexities of organizational demands, interpersonal dynamics, and ethical reasoning in order to achieve the greater good. However, little research has been done on the topic of how organizational dynamics foster deception. Thus, the study at the core of this book was conducted through an interdisciplinary approach guided by the theoretical frameworks of organizational analysis, social psychology, and ethical decision-making. This presentation of theories of organizational analysis supports the thesis that neither people nor organizations operate out of any single set of driving principles. Organizations, and the people in them, operate from driving forces that can best be understood from a variety of perspectives—as presented in chapters 2, 3, and 4. The results can be summarized into the following eight findings:

1. School administrators interact daily with students, teachers, support staff, parents, other administrators, and central office personnel, all of whom expect to find resolutions to their problems from the school administrator; however, these expectations cannot always be met.

2. Less-than-honest behavior may be perceived as the only way to

manage the conflicting demands of all the populations school administrators serve.

3. The types of organizational dynamics that create ethically compromising situations for school administrators were identified as emerging from:

   (a) the structural dynamics of maintaining productivity, protecting children, influencing decisions, and protecting resources;

   (b) the personal dynamics of making personal judgments, dealing with cultural differences, protecting staff, and protecting personal and organizational priorities;

   (c) the interpersonal dynamics of hidden agendas, sanctions, conflict and conflict avoidance, and group norms;

   (d) the cultural dynamics of intolerant superintendents, organizational sanctions, some aspects of socialization, issues of cultural diversity, and problematic organizational norms; and,

   (e) the political dynamics of interests, power, and resources.

4. The types of less-than-honest behavior school administrators used to manage the conflicting demands of the populations they serve were as follows:

   (a) as a result of *structural dynamics*, forging documentation or results, bending or ignoring rules, hiding funds, manipulating procedures, ignoring policy, and withholding information or using ambiguous language;

   (b) as a result of *personal dynamics*, lying to protect others, compromising to benefit others, compromising to avoid conflict, and treating people differently;

   (c) as a result of *interpersonal dynamics*, hiding bad news, accepting negative situations, disregarding public laws, disregarding supervisory responsibilities, disregarding student rights, failing to inform parents of student issues, excluding others from public process, and ignoring district policy and procedure;

   (d) as a result of *cultural dynamics*, misrepresenting self, accepting situations perceived as negative, hiding bad news, disregarding public laws, engaging in strategic ambiguity, and treating people differently based on race;

(e) as a result of *political dynamics*, altering letters of recommendation, keeping bad news hidden from both central office and parents, misrepresenting self, withholding information at another's expense, hiding funds, and lying for what is considered right.

5. The categories of less-than-honest behaviors most widely engaged in from all five perspectives of the organizational analysis are hiding bad news, hiding funds, and engaging in differential treatment.

6. The same types of less-than-honest behaviors were used to respond to the social/psychological dynamics of mentoring, individual perceptions, avoiding conflict, protecting others, and group norms.

7. The ethical bases and the types of reasoning school administrators used to manage their pressures were found to be as follows:

(a) although a Platonic sense of ethics was a guiding principle in the ethical reasoning on the part of one participant, she and others acknowledged that political pressures and organizational limitations often made it too difficult to follow all of the rules or work to change them;

(b) a Humean sense of ethics was a major component of one participant's ethical reasoning and was applied primarily in the protection and benefiting of self;

(c) a Kantian sense of ethics was not a component of the ethical reasoning in which any participants engaged;

(d) a Millsian sense of ethics was one of the two most common bases from which the participants drew in meeting the needs of others;

(e) an approach based on respect for persons, from the work of Downie and Telfer, was the other most common basis for ethical decision-making.

8. The less-than-honest behaviors of ignoring policy, bending or breaking rules, withholding information, and lying (solely for the benefit of others) were perceived as ethically rational and justifiable humanistic responses to compromising situations.

CONCLUSIONS

These school administrators have eloquently described the challenges and personal turmoil they face when trying to act responsibly toward their organizations and the people they serve. Their concerns, more often than not, had to do with issues of individuality, problematic rules and redefined roles, and racial differences. Their interview responses also offered evidence of a body of knowledge that can be described as the wisdom of professional practice.

The findings of the study have led to four major conclusions regarding the nature of less-than-honest behavior in the professional practice of school administrators. The four conclusions are discussed under the headings of (a) the administrator as person, (b) rules and roles, (c) professional practice, and (d) cultural differences.

The Administrator as Person

This study found that all of the participants use less-than-honest behavior to mediate the conflicts of their work. It also found, perhaps surprisingly, that individuals will admit to more than white lies. This study further determined that the majority of untruths told by the participants were not told to benefit themselves or to save face, but rather to benefit or protect others.

This study also supports research that suggests individuals can be active creators of their own scripts and roles and define their own characters. Indeed, the longer the participants had been administrators, the more they bent or ignored specific rules and redefined their roles in regard to doing what they felt necessary to meet the individual needs of others, especially students.

The interview responses indicate that the participants used ethical reasoning to negotiate the ethical compromises resulting from the conflicting demands of the populations they serve. One troublesome finding is that, although one of the participants held the Platonic ideal of working to change rules rather than break them, more of them acknowledged that political pressures and organizational limitations often precluded their following all the rules or working to change them.

In fact, one participant reported that he was politically damaged as a result of speaking out and trying to change district practices regarding loyalty and positional power. Another reported that she, too, suffered political sanctions as a result of following district procedures. These findings suggest that some informal organizational norms actually deter honest communication and compliance with the bureaucracy.

Although most of the participants acknowledged their commitment to doing the right thing for the right reasons, none of them hinted that their practice would be a good example for everybody to follow. Rather, a general acknowledgment was apparent that such practices—although necessary—were individual, painful, and undiscussable.

The two most common bases from which the participants drew their ethical reasoning were Mill's theory and Downie and Telfer's theory in which striving for the greater good and respect for persons are the bases for decision-making. Interestingly, participants acknowledged that individuals' needs often cannot be met through, and are frequently hurt by, following district policy and procedure.

Rules and Roles

Because not all members of a community have the same goals, conflict is inherent in the making and keeping of rules. Furthermore, the reality is that all policies are not created equal, and they aren't interpreted equally. The making of policies and rules can be a rational process in response to the needs of a community; just as often, the making of policies and rules can occur in response to political pressures.

The manner in which the participants followed specific rules depended upon the context and on how the rules were regarded. Some rules were thought to be vague, open to interpretation, and therefore bendable; other rules were perceived as precise, not open to interpretation, and therefore to be either followed or broken. As some of these interviewees noted, precise rules often are not sensitive to the needs of individuals. Some also described the difficulties of making independent judgments when rules are vague.

From the top of the school district hierarchy, the superintendent might well look down on perceived order and uniformity and observe a well-organized structure of tasks and responsibilities in which the principal's job is to efficiently carry out the policies and procedures of the district. From the bottom, students and teachers might look up at a group of school- and district-level administrators and see people whose job is to help meet the needs of individuals. In the middle is the school principal, whose job is to serve in the classic bind of middle management that is to meet the often-conflicting demands of the individuals and groups in the organization.

In terms of the school district hierarchy, participants spoke of having their actions or opinions evaluated by higher-ups, who then made decisions that either limited or allowed resources, responsibilities, and power to reach the principals. The participants described these vertically driven, authority-based processes as impediments they were compelled to work around in order to meet the needs of their students and teachers.

In other words, the rules by which school administrators are expected to work are often in conflict with a major portion of their roles. In response to this conflict, these participants report what can be seen, from one perspective, as engaging in unethical or illegal behavior. Rather than accepting the limitations of their roles, these participants are creating, as described by one participant, "alternate ways of operating," which, from another perspective, are necessary "to meet the needs of the students," "to show parents that the school cares," and "to keep the school from becoming progressively poorer and poorer."

Genuine authority derives its power from legitimacy; the same is true of rules. Rules also depend on context, and adherence to them is always in a state of flux. In terms of this study, specific rules weren't followed if the participants didn't believe in them. Tasks, too, were performed depending on whether they were clearly laid out or ambiguous. The results of these interviews suggest a similarity among the organizational components of authority, rules, and tasks. Candid responses from the participants show that some of them felt it necessary to assume the authority to follow some rules and not others, and to define their tasks in ways that protected their constituents on one side of the hierarchy, but potentially damaged their status with their constituents on the other side.

The fact that the majority of these participants report such behavior in their professional practice reinforces a major conclusion of this study: that *a conflict exists between the roles and tasks of school administrators*. It also looks as if, to some extent at least, these participants are redefining their roles and their tasks in response to that conflict. As a result of their motivation and experience, these administrators seem to be going beyond the rational model of administrative decision-making: they are increasingly moving past the expectations of others and creating their own, more intuitive criteria for being effective administrators. It is possible that school administrators, in moving beyond the limited rational model of administrative decision-making, are creating new administrative roles—indeed a new professional practice—based on their individual ethical reasoning and professional wisdom.

Professional Practice

The ethical issues of justice and student welfare are always present in the process of developing and maintaining a school community. This means that school administrators must find ways to apply ethical reasoning to both vague and precise rules. Ethical reasoning, ethical judgments, and ethical actions are the foundation from which school principals can sort out the issues of justice and student welfare that lie at the heart of building a school community.

All of the interviewees said they felt uneasy when withholding information. Perhaps it could be acknowledged that it's necessary for administrators to refrain from full disclosure in specific situations, thereby reducing the tension these administrators feel. If there were an acknowledged policy whereby administrators could withhold information in particular situations, they wouldn't have to rely on the distressing need to make ongoing individual judgments about when to refrain from telling the whole truth.

Research shows that school administrators go through stages of socialization. The first stage can include moving into and accepting the school's social setting. This study suggests that this phase does indeed exist.

The two least-experienced administrators reported efforts at making sense of the school's culture and fitting in. One of them said she made various compromises, based on what team members said, in order to fit in and to build trust. The newcomer said of negative circumstances, "I came to grips with it and realized that that's the way life is, and there's not anything I can do about it so I might just as well accept it." Other participants reported "looking for the mold to fit in," "looking for the ways others are successful," and "not saying anything that might jeopardize my career."

The complicated nature of this stage is poignantly addressed by one of the newer participants, who reported, "I don't think we give anybody up-front advice. Before you take a position, somebody needs to tell you, 'This is the culture.' You need to pay attention to the culture of the environment the minute you walk in." The irony is that to the degree that new administrators accept the position as it is, they will be unable to establish themselves and make changes—to respond in a way that reflects how they wish to be seen.

It has been suggested that once an administrator has moved into the second stage by becoming an established part of the organizational "scene," people no longer expect that person to make changes. However, most of the participants in this study expressed the desire and commitment to work toward increased autonomy and professional skill in an effort to meet the needs of others. Career maintenance alone was not considered enough; participants discussed the importance of career meaning. These administrators reported making important alterations in the way they do their work in order to fulfill their role of benefiting students.

A third stage can be called the stabilization stage. Some suggest that this phase consists of making a recommitment to organizational goals. The results of this study, however, don't support that notion. The two principals with the most experience, both of whom are within a few years of retirement, talked about being committed to the professional goals of helping children and meeting the needs of individuals—even at the expense of attaining organizational goals.

The interviews support the notion that group norms tend to develop as the result of statements by supervisors or colleagues. Most of the participants expressed a direct connection between some types of less-than-honest behavior and statements from their supervisors that "bad news is not wanted." The participants reported that, as a result of such statements, they hid bad news, manipulated test scores, made various compromises, and accepted negative situations. The interview responses also indicate that some group norms not only work against honest communication, but also can lead to overt deception, as indicated by reports from the participants that cheating on standardized test procedures has emerged as a norm in their districts.

The finding that statements by superiors have an effect upon group norms reinforces research showing that organizational leaders are responsible for structures and routines that lead to increased organizational productivity and efficiency. Accordingly, findings from this study dispute previous research suggesting that the organization's culture is more influential than is its management. Many of the participants reported that their approaches to conflict management were based on the strong messages from their superintendents that no bad news was wanted. Administrators reported feeling that the security of their position was based on their fitting in or appearing to fit in. It would seem that superintendents have much more influence on principals' behavior and the district's culture than they, the superintendents, perhaps suspect.

The results of these interviews suggest that the superintendent greatly influences the principals' perceptions of acceptable practices. Therefore, it would be wise of superintendents to conscientiously match their behaviors to their spoken and written statements. On the other hand, superintendents might recognize the types of deception in which their principals are engaged, and might, therefore, for political reasons, choose to ignore the issue because of benefits to children, schools, communities, and, perhaps, the superintendents themselves.

Superintendents, therefore, appear to have two options when they catch principals engaging in less-than-honest behavior. They can ignore the issue and tolerate the gap between approved policy and what is actually being accomplished that might not otherwise be able to be accomplished. Or, they can focus on developing a closer match between approved policy and procedure and what principals actually do.

The reality that all five participants candidly described the manner in which they use less-than-honest behavior, and identified such less-than-honest behavior as part of the norms of their culture, even to the degree of being mentored to use less-than-honest behavior, suggests that different types of less-than-honest behavior, in response to various motivations, is unquestionably a part of the organizational culture of these five school principals. The common understandings around which this group of participants organized their actions were, according to the various perspectives of analysis, the needs to protect others, the organization, and self.

Nothing in this study contradicts the results of previous research suggesting that groups, their differences, and the scarcity of resources will always lead to conflict and political forces. As Plutarch wrote, "[Politics] is not a public chore, to be got over with; it is a way of life." Indeed, all of the participants identified and described coalitions they supported and coalitions they tried to destroy. They described the differences of beliefs, values, and perceptions of reality of groups and individuals in their schools and districts. And they described the scarcity of resources in their buildings and district budgets, the conflict that resulted, and the various compromises that constitute the political reality of their work.

Cultural Differences

When minority groups in schools were discussed, it was frequently in terms of ways in which they didn't match up with the dominant culture. The control of schools by the dominant culture gives it power that other groups don't have. Socialization through schools can be viewed as a powerful tool for giving society the shape that the dominant culture wants it to have. Examined from this perspective, racism and schools can appear to be tightly interconnected. As one of the participants said, "In order to keep minority kids in school, you have to make allowances, and the allowance can't be that you have increased their reading scores, so you have to allow minority kids more latitude in the way they conduct themselves." This comment suggests that the dominant culture continues to identify cultural differences as a problem of the minority's deficiencies rather than one of white racism.

The cultural and political reality of the treatment of minorities by the dominant culture is one of the major issues facing America and its school system. The interaction among dominant and minority cultures is, according to these administrators, a troublesome source of less-than-honest behavior in schools. For example, a current approach to bridging the cultural gap is to hire more minority teachers. The logic behind the approach seems to be that minority teachers are likely to be more sensitive to the needs of minority students. Although one participant suggested that making and acting upon this assumption gets people from the dominant culture off the hook in terms of examining the holes in their own worldview, another assumed that a minority would "get the job because she is black." Another suggested that the hiring of minorities is avoided "because of the extra supervisory responsibilities" associated with minority hires.

What is real, according to these participants, is that administrators are taught to treat minorities differently, and that they pass that teaching along to new administrators. One participant reported the common belief that minority teachers require more supervision and guidance than do nonminorities. Another reported being mentored to treat minority students as academically and behaviorally less capable than white students. Four participants acknowledged that organizational responses to racial differences create situations in which it is impossible to respond honestly.

More encouragingly, three participants indicated that their experiences with minorities and discrimination improved the way they viewed cultural differences, suggesting that more interaction between school principals and minorities would be helpful in counteracting what appear to be prevalent norms of differential treatment. If this is true—if principals are hiding resources and bad news, and engaging in differential treatment based on race—then the implications for site-based management, which is predicated on the open and honest exchange of information about resources, shared power, and not altogether exclusive interests, are daunting.

RECOMMENDATIONS

The following recommendations come from the careful consideration of the literature from the three broad areas of organizational theory, social psychology, and ethical decision-making, and from the findings and conclusions derived from the interviews collected for this study. Because the participants were so few in number, and because of their professional status, geographic location, and cultural backgrounds, it is not my intent to generalize the findings and conclusions of the present study as representative of all school administrators. Although these findings cannot be generalized, they do suggest some considerations by professional associations, district superintendents, university training programs, and researchers.

First, confronted with the conflicts and ethical compromises inherent in their middle-management roles, school principals may well need the support of professional associations to help identify some aspects of their role as more important than others. It is recommended, therefore, that professional associations examine the roles of school administrators and then articulate, at a national level, whether those roles that relate directly to meeting the needs of students supersede other organizational roles.

Second, given that superintendents appear to have a strong influence on principals' perceptions of acceptable practices, it seems important for superintendents to carefully and consciously match their behaviors to their spoken and written statements.

Third, university preparation programs would do well to offer more meaningful and detailed education in organizational culture, racial and cultural differences, and dealing with conflict. Participants clearly articulated their need for more help in those areas. Specifically, administrative training programs could prepare and present course work in organizational analysis, focusing especially on the areas of politics and organizational culture. If school administrators are expected to lead efforts in school reform, including site-based management, administrative trainees need the theoretical and practical understanding of organizational dynamics. Additionally, such training programs could prepare and present course work on cultural differences. Regularly treating minorities differently, as the interviewees described, leads only to well-known destructive outcomes.

Finally, too little is known about the logic of the normative, political, and moral judgments made by school administrators. More research is necessary to find out just how widespread such behavior is.

Moreover, additional research could help us learn whether or not the link this study noted between the behavior of superintendents and their principals is present among other administrators in other settings. It would also help to clarify whether there is a similar link between the ethical practices of principals and teachers and/or students in the same school.

SUMMARY

Clearly, the onus of less-than-honest behavior rests not only on the individual; organizational situations and pressures do come into play. When all news has to be good news, when resources are inadequate to support district initiatives, or when district initiatives do not take cultural realties into account, organizational dynamics can result in less-than-honest administrative behavior. In addition, this study suggests that the school administrator's role of protecting the interests of others often conflicts with the rules of the organization. In such situations, less-than-honest behavior is sometimes perceived as the most humane and compassionate choice available. That is why school administrators sometimes resort to using it.

So here you are, the newly hired school administrator. You have been selected for a leadership position at a critical time for K–12 education. You are a person of integrity. You have excellent interpersonal and organizational skills. To deceive others is so far from what is in your mind that it is unimaginable. And yet, based on what these five school administrators tell us, what you have learned as a basic moral code ("thou shalt not lie") lies in direct contradiction to what is known of justice ("protect the powerless"), and is certain to become an issue of organizational rewards, or even survival ("don't make waves"). It is even possible for the work itself to feel so different from what you expected that you might find yourself questioning just exactly who you are. How will you decide?

Bibliography

Alinsky, S. (1971). *Rules for radicals*. New York: Random House.

Argyris, C. (1986). Skilled incompetence. *Harvard Business Review*, September/October, 74–79.

Aron, A., & Aron, E. (1989). *The heart of social psychology* (2nd ed.). Lexington, MA: D. C. Heath.

Ayer, A. J. (1952). *Language, truth and logic*. New York: Dover Publications, Inc.

Baird, J. E., & Weinberg, S. B. (1981). *Group communication: The essence of synergy* (2nd ed.). Dubuque, IA: Wm. C. Brown Company.

Baird, L., & Kram, K. E. (1986). Career dynamics: Managing the superior/subordinate relationship. *Organizational Dynamics, 11*, 46–64.

Baker-Miller, J. (1976). Domination–Subordination. In *Toward a new psychology of women* (pp. 3–12). Boston: Beacon Press.

Baldwin, J. (1952). *Go tell it on the mountain*. New York: Doubleday.

Bandura, A. (1977). *Social learning theory*. Englewood Cliffs, NJ: Prentice Hall.

Barnett, R., & Baruch, G. (1980). On being an economic provider: Women's involvement in multiple roles. In D. McGuigan (Ed.), *Women's lives: New theory, research, policy* (pp. 47–64). Ann Arbor: University of Michigan Center for Continuing Education of Women.

Bass, B. (1990). *Bass and Stogdill's handbook of leadership*. New York: The Free Press.

Bauchner, J. E., Brandt, D. R., & Miller, G. R. (1977). The truth/deception attribution: Effects of varying levels of information availability. In B. R. Ruben (Ed.), *Communication yearbook 1* (pp. 229–243). New Brunswick, NJ: Transaction Books.

Bauchner, J. E., Kaplan, E. P., & Miller, G. R. (1980). Detecting deception: The relationship of available information to judgmental accuracy in initial encounters. *Human Communication Research, 6*, 251–264.

Bennett, J. T., & DiLorenzo, T. J. (1992). *Official lies: How Washington misleads us.* Alexandria, VA: Groom Books.

Berlo, D. K., Lemert, J. B., & Mertz, R. J. (1969–1970). Dimensions for evaluating the acceptability of message sources. *Public Opinion Quarterly, 33,* 563–576.

Black, H. C. (1991). *Black's law dictionary* (abridged 6th ed.). St. Paul, MN: West Publishing Company.

Bloom, B. S. (1953). Thought processes in lectures and discussions. *Journal of General Education, 7,* 160–169.

Bogdan, R. C., & Biklen, S. K. (1982). *Qualitative research for education: An introduction to theory and methods.* Boston: Allyn & Bacon.

Bok, S. (1979). *Lying: Moral choice in public and private life.* New York: Vintage.

Bok, S. (1982). *Secrets.* New York: Pantheon.

Bolman, L. G., & Deal, T. E. (1991). *Reframing organizations: Artistry, choice, and leadership.* San Francisco: Jossey-Bass.

Brandt, D. R., Miller, G. R., & Hocking, J. E. (1980a). Effects of self-monitoring and familiarity on deception detection. *Communication Quarterly, 28,* 3–10.

Brandt, D. R., Miller, G. R., & Hocking, J. E. (1980b). The truth deception attribution: Effects of familiarity on the ability of observers to detect deception. *Human Communication Research, 6,* 99–110.

Brandt, D. R., Miller, G. R., & Hocking, J. E. (1982). Familiarity and lie detection: A replication and extension. *Western Journal of Speech Communication, 46,* 276–290.

Brown, C. (1963). *Manchild in the promised land.* New York: Signet.

Buller, D. B., Comstock, J., Aune, R. K., & Strzyzewski, K. D. (1989). The effect of probing on deceivers and truthtellers. *Journal of Nonverbal Behavior, 13,* 155–170.

Buller, D. B., Strzyzewski, K. D., & Comstock, J. (1991). Interpersonal Deception I: Deceiver's reactions to receiver's suspicions and probing. *Communication Monographs, 58,* 1–24.

Burns, J. M. (1978). *Leadership.* New York: Harper & Row.

Camden, C., Motley, M. T., & Wilson, A. (1984). White lies in interpersonal communication. *Western Journal of Speech Communication, 48* (4), 309–325.

Carroll, M. G. (2001). *Exploring the relationship between organizational commitment and employee beliefs, expectations, and experiences of mission in a values-based organization.* Unpublished dissertation, Gonzaga University, Spokane, WA.

Cavalli-Sforza, L., Menozzi, P., & Piazza, A. (1994). *The history and geography of human genes.* Princeton, NJ: Princeton University Press.

Clark, B. R. (1960). The "cooling-out" function in higher education. *American Journal of Sociology,* May, 569 576.

Clarke, K. (2001). *Last things first.* Keynote address at the conference, "So Now What? Beyond the Clichés of Leadership," Spokane, WA, October 25, 26.

Cody, M. J., Marsten, P. J., & Foster, M. (1984). Deception: Paralinguistic and verbal leakage. In R. N. Bostrum (Ed.), *Communication Yearbook* (pp. 464–490). Beverly Hills, CA: Sage.

Cody, M. J., & O'Hair, H. D. (1983). Nonverbal communication and deception: Differences in deception cues due to gender and communicator dominance. *Communication Monographs, 50,* 175–192.

Cytrynbaum, S., & Crites, J. O. (1989). The utility of adult development theory in understanding career adjustment process. In Arthur, Hall, & Lawrence (Eds.), *Handbook of career therapy* (pp. 66–88). Cambridge: Cambridge University Press.

Deal, T. E., & Kennedy, A. (1982). *Corporate cultures.* Reading, MA: Addison-Wesley.

Deigh, J. (1992). *Ethics and personality: Essays in moral psychology.* Chicago: University of Chicago Press.

DePaulo, B. M., Kirkendol, S. E., Tang, J., & O'Brien, T. (1988). The motivational impairment effect in the communication of deception: Replications and extensions. *Journal of Nonverbal Behavior, 12,* 177–202.

DePaulo, B. M., Zuckerman, M., & Rosenthal, R. (1980). Humans as lie detectors. *Journal of Communication, 30,* 129–139.

Deutsch, M. (1949). A theory of cooperation and competition. *Human Relations, 2,* 129–152.

Deutsch, M. (1973). *The resolution of conflict.* New Haven, CT: Yale University Press.

Deutsch, M. & Krauss, R. M. (1965). *Theories in social psychology.* New York: Basic Books.

Diamond, M. A. (1991). Stresses of group membership: Balancing the needs for independence and belonging. In M. F. R. Kets de Vries, *Organizations on the couch: Clinical perspectives on organizational behavior and change* (pp. 191–213). San Francisco: Jossey-Bass.

Downie, R. S., Loudfoot, E., & Telfer, E. (1974). *Education and personal relationships.* London: Methuen and Company.

Downie, R. S., & Telfer, E. (1969). *Respect for persons.* London: Allen & Unwin.

Eck, M. (1970). *Lies and truth.* London: Collier-Macmillan.

Ecklein, J. (1982). Women in the German Democratic Republic: Impact of culture and social policy. In J. Geile (Ed.), *Women in the middle years* (pp. 129–141). New York: Wiley.

Ekman, P. (1985). *Telling lies: Clues to deceit in the marketplace, politics, and marriage.* New York: W. W. Norton & Company.

Ekman, P. (1992). *Telling lies: Clues to deceit in the marketplace, politics, and marriage.* New York: W. W. Norton & Company.

Ekman, P., & Friesen, W. V. (1974). Detecting deception from the body or face. *Journal of Personality and Social Psychology, 20,* 288–298.

Elliott, G. C. (1979). Some effects of deception and level of self-monitoring on planning and reacting to a self-presentation. *Journal of Personality and Social Psychology, 37,* 1282, 1292.

Ellis, H. C. (1972). *Fundamentals of human learning and cognition.* Dubuque, IA: Wm. C. Brown Company.

Ellison, R. (1947). *Invisible man.* New York: Random House.

Elstein, A. S., Shulman, L. S., & Sprafka, A. S. (1978). *Medical problem-solving: An analysis of clinical reasoning.* Cambridge, MA: Harvard University Press.

Erikson, E. (1968). *Identity, youth, and crisis.* New York: W. W. Norton.

Etzioni, A. (1988). *The moral dimension: Toward a new economics.* New York: Free Press.

Feldman, D. C. (1985). Diagnosing and changing group norms. *1985 Annual: Developing Human Resources,* 72–79.

Feldman, R. S. (1983, April). *In defense of children's lies: On ethics and methods of studying children's communication of deception.* Paper presented at the meeting of the American Educational Research Association, Montreal, Canada.

Feldman, R. S. (Ed.). (1982). *Development of nonverbal behavior in children.* New York: Springer.

Feldman, R. S., & White, J. B. (1980). Detecting deception in children. *Journal of Communication, 30,* 121–128.

Fink, A., & Kosecoff, J. (1985). *How to conduct surveys.* Newbury Park, CA: Sage.

Flam, H. (1993). Fear, loyalty and greedy organizations. In S. Fineman (Ed.), *Emotion in organizations* (pp. 58–75). Newbury Park, CA: Sage.

Forsyth, B. H., & Lessler, J. T. (1992). Cognitive laboratory methods: A taxonomy. In P. N. Biemer, R. N. Groves, L. E. Lyberg, N. A. Mathiowetz, & S. Sudman (Eds.), *Measurement errors in surveys* (pp. 393–418). New York: John Wiley.

Fowler, F. J. (1993). *Survey research methods.* Newbury Park, CA: Sage.

Frank, R. H. (1988). *Passions within reason: The strategic role of the emotions.* New York: W. W. Norton.

Frankfurt, H. G. (2005). *On Bullshit.* Princeton, NJ: Princeton University Press.

French, J. R. P., & Raven, B. (1959). The bases of social power. In D. Cartwright (Ed.), *Studies in social power* (pp. 150–167). Ann Arbor: University of Michigan, Institute for Social Research.

Freud, S. (1953–1966). *The standard edition of the complete works of Sigmund Freud* (J. Strachey, Trans.). London: Hogarth Press.

Freud, S. (1961). *The ego and the id.* (J. Strachey, Trans.). New York: W. W. Norton & Co.

Frohlich, N., & Oppenheimer, J. A. (1992). *Choosing justice: An experimental approach to ethical theory.* Berkeley: University of California Press.

Gagné, R. M. (1971). *Conditions of learning.* New York: Holt, Rinehart and Winston.

Gallos, J. V. (1989). Exploring women's development: Implications for career theory, practice, and research. In B. Arthur, D. Hall, & B. Lawrence (Eds.), *Handbook of career therapy* (pp. 110–132). Cambridge: Cambridge University Press.

Gamoran, A., & Dreeben, R. (1986). Coupling and control in educational organizations. *Administrative Science Quarterly, 31,* 612–632.

Gilligan, C. (1982). *In a different voice: Psychological theory and women's development.* Cambridge, MA: Harvard University Press.

Glaser, B., & Strauss, A. (1967). *Discovery of grounded theory.* Chicago: Aldine Press.

Gouldner, A. W. (1960). The reciprocity norm: A preliminary statement. *American Sociological Review, 25,* 161–178.

Greene, J. O., O'Hair, D., Cody, M. J., & Yen, C. (1985). Planning and control of behavior during deception. *Human Communication Research, 11,* 335–364.

Greenleaf, R. S. (1973). *The servant as leader*. Petersborough, NH: Center for Applied Sciences.

Greenleaf, R. S. (1977). *Servant leadership*. New York: Paulist Press.

Grove, R. W. (1988). An analysis of the constant comparative method. *Qualitative Studies in Education, 1* (3), 273–279.

Guba, E. G. (1978). *Toward a methodology of naturalistic inquiry in educational evaluation*. Los Angeles: University of California, Graduate School of Education, Center for the Study of Evaluation.

Hamburg, D. A. (1992). *Today's children: Creating a future for a generation in crisis*. New York: Random House.

Hample, D. (1980). Purposes and effects of lying. *Southern Speech Communication Journal, 46,* 33–47.

Hample, D. (1982). *Empirical evidence for a typology of lies*. Paper presented at the meeting of the Speech Communication Association, Louisville, KY.

Handel, T. H. (1982). Intelligence. *Journal of Strategic Studies, 5,* 179–185.

Hart, A. W. (1991). Leader succession and socialization: A synthesis. *Review of Educational Research, 61* (4), 451–474.

Haslam, S. A., Platow, M. J., Turner, J. C., Reynolds, K. J., McGarty, C., Oakes, P. J., Johnson, S., Ryan, M. K., & Veenstra, K. (2001). Social identity and the romance of leadership: The importance of being seen to be "doing it for us." *Group Processes & Intergroup Relations, 4* (3), 191–205.

Helgesen, S. (1990). *The female advantage*. Doubleday: New York.

Hennestad, B. W. (1990). The symbolic impact of double bind leadership: Double bind and the dynamics of organizational culture. *Journal of Management Studies, 27* (3), 265, 280.

Hewlett, S. A. (1991). *When the bough breaks: The cost of neglecting our children*. New York: Basic Books.

Hocking, J. E., Bauchner, J., Kaminski, E. P., & Miller, G. R. (1979). Detecting deceptive communication from verbal, visual, and paralinguistic cues. *Human Communication Research, 6,* 33–46.

Hoefnagels, C., & Zwikker, M. (2001). The bystander dilemma and child abuse: Extending the Latane and Darley model to domestic violence. *Journal of Applied Social Psychology, 31* (6), 1158–1183.

Hogan, R., Raskin, R., & Fazzini, D. (1990). How charisma cloaks incompetence. *Personnel Journal, 69* (5), 73–76.

Hume, D. (1983). *An enquiry concerning the principles of morals*. Indianapolis, IN: Hackett. (original work published 1751)

Hurston, Z. N. (1990). *Their eyes were watching God.* New York: Harper & Row.

Iles, G. (2005). *Turning angel.* New York: Scribner.

Jacobs, J. (1992). *Systems of survival.* New York: Random House.

Jordan, W. (1969). *White over black.* Baltimore, MD: Penguin Books.

Justice, P. L. (1987, November). *"What she doesn't know won't hurt her": Gender effects on patterns of interpersonal deception.* Paper presented at the annual meeting of the Speech Communication Association, Boston.

Kagan, N. (1972). *Influencing human interaction.* ERIC Document Reproduction Service No. ED 065 793.

Kagan, N. (1973). *Influencing human interaction: Eleven years of interpersonal process recall.* Paper presented at the annual meeting of the American Educational Research Association, New Orleans.

Kagan, N., Krathwohl, D. R., & Miller, R. (1963). Stimulated recall in therapy: A case study. *Journal of Counseling Psychology, 10,* 237–243.

Kant, I. (1981). *Grounding for the metaphysics of morals.* (J. W. Ellington, Trans.). Indianapolis, IN: Hackett. (original work published 1785)

Kanter, R. M. (1983). *The change masters.* New York: Simon & Schuster.

Katz, D., & Kahn, R. (1975). Organizational change: Individual and small group. In J. V. Baldridge & T. E. Deal (Eds.), *Managing change in educational organizations: Sociological perspectives, strategies, and case studies.* Berkeley, CA: McCutchan Publishing Co.

Keating, C. (1993). Relationship between dominance and deception among adult men. *Journal of Social Issues, 3,* 635–647.

Keele, R. (1986). Mentoring or networking? Strong and weak ties in career development. In L. Moore (Ed.), *Not as far as you think: The realities of working women* (pp. 130–146). Lexington, MA: Lexington.

Keith, M. J. (1988). *Stimulated recall and teachers' thought processes: A critical review of the methodology and an alternative perspective.* Paper presented at the annual meeting of the Mid-South Educational Research Association, Louisville, KY.

Keller, F. S. (1969). *Learning: Reinforcement theory.* New York: Random House.

Kelley, H. H. (1967). Attribution theory in social psychology. In D. Levine (Ed.), *Nebraska Symposium on Motivation* (pp. 135–147). Lincoln: University of Nebraska Press.

Kelley, H. H. (1979). *Personal relationships: Their structures and processes.* Hillsdale, NJ: Lawrence Erlbaum.

Kelley, H. H., Berscheid, E., Christensen, A., Harvey, J. H., Huston, T. L., Lev-
inger, G., McClintock, E., Peplau, L. A., & Peterson, D. R. (1983). *Close
relationships.* New York: Freeman.

Kelley, H. H., & Thibaut, J. W. (1978). *Interpersonal relations: A theory of interdependence.* New York: Wiley-Interscience.

Kets de Vries, M. F. R. (1991). *Organizations on the couch: Clinical perspectives
on organizational behavior and change.* San Francisco: Jossey-Bass.

Kilmann, R. H., & Saxton, M. J. (1983). *Organizational cultures: Their assessment and change.* San Francisco: Jossey-Bass.

Kimbrough, R. B. (1985). *Ethics: A course of study for educational leaders.* Ar-
lington, VA: American Association of School Administrators.

Klockars, C. B. (1984). Blue lies and police placebos: The morality of police
lying. *American Behavioral Scientist, 27* (4), 529–544.

Knapp, M. L., & Comadena, M. E. (1979). Telling it like it isn't: A review of
theory and research on deceptive communications. *Human Communication
Research, 5,* 270–285.

Koffka, K. (1929). *The growth of the mind* (2nd ed.). New York: Harcourt Brace
Jovanovich.

Koffka, K. (1935). *Principles of gestalt psychology.* New York: Harcourt Brace
Jovanovich.

Kohlberg, L. (1976). Moral stages and moralization: The cognitive-develop-
mental approach. In T. Lickona (Ed.), *Moral development and behavior:
Theory, research and social issues.* New York: Holt, Rinehart and Winston.

Köhler, W. (1929). *Gestalt psychology.* New York: McKay.

Koontz, D. (2000). *Dark rivers of the heart.* New York: Bantam.

Koper, R. J., & Sahlman, J. M. (1991, May). *The behavioral correlates of real-
world deceptive communication.* Paper presented at the meeting of the International Communication Association, Chicago.

Krauss, R. M., Apple, W., Morency, N., Wenzel, C., & Winston, W. (1981).
Verbal, vocal, and visible factors in judgments of another's effect. *Journal of
Personality and Social Psychology, 40,* 312–320.

LaBier, D. (1986). *Modern madness: The emotional fallout of success.* Reading,
MA: Addison-Wesley.

Lasswell, H. D. (1958). *Politics: Who gets what, when, and how.* Cleveland, OH:
Meridian Books.

Lepage, M.A. (1993). *The Kafkesque organization.* Online publication. [http://
qlink.queensu.ca/~3mal5/kafkesque.html]

Lerner, A. W., & Wanat, J. (1983). Fuzziness and bureaucracy. *Public Administrator Review, 43* (6), 500–509.

Lessler, J., & Tourangeau, R. (1989). Questionnaire design in the cognitive research laboratory. *Vital and Health Statistics, 6,* 1. Washington, DC: Government Printing Office.

Levinson, D. J. (1978). *The seasons of a man's life.* New York: Knopf.

Lewin, K. (1935). *A dynamic theory of personality.* New York: McGraw-Hill.

Lewin, K. (1936). *Principles of topological psychology.* New York: McGraw-Hill.

Lewin, K. (1951). *Field theory in social science.* New York: Harper & Row.

Likert, R. (1967). *The human organization.* New York: McGraw-Hill.

Lincoln, Y. S., & Guba, E. G. (1983). *Naturalistic inquiry.* Beverly Hills, CA: Sage.

Lindzey, G., & Aronsen, E. (Eds.). (1980). *The handbook of social psychology* (3rd ed.). New York: Random House.

Loevinger, J. (1976). *Ego development: Conceptions and theories.* San Francisco: Jossey-Bass.

Louis, M. R. (1980). Surprise and sense making. *Administrative Science Quarterly, 25,* 226, 251.

Louis, M. R. (1985). An investigator's guide to workplace culture. In P. Frost et al. (Eds.), *Organizational culture* (pp. 73–93). Beverly Hills, CA: Sage.

Ludwig, A. M. (1965). *The importance of lying.* Springfield, IL: Charles C. Thomas.

Lyth, I. M. (1991). Changing organizations and individuals: Psychoanalytic insights for improving organizational health. In M. F. R. Kets de Vries, *Organizations on the couch: Clinical perspectives on organizational behavior and change* (pp. 361–378). San Francisco: Jossey-Bass.

Maadi, S. R. (1980). *Personality theories: A comparative analysis.* Homewood, IL: Dorsey Press.

Machiavelli, N. (1513; 1966). *The prince.* New York: Bantam Books.

Marshall, C., & Rossman, G. B. (1989). *Designing qualitative research.* Newbury Park, CA: Sage.

Martin, M. (1990). *The keys of this blood.* New York: Simon & Schuster.

May, R. (1972). *Power and innocence.* New York: W. W. Norton & Co.

McClelland, D. C. (1985). *Human motivation.* Glenview, IL: Scott, Foresman.

McCornack, S. A. (1992). Information manipulation theory. *Communication Monographs, 59* (1), 1–16.

McCornack, S. A., & Levine, T. R. (1990). When lies are uncovered: Emotional and relational outcomes of discovered deception. *Communication Monographs, 57* (2), 119–138.

McCornack, S. A., & Parks, M. R. (1986). Deception detection and relational development: The other side of trust. In M. L. McLaughlin (Ed.), *Communication yearbook 9* (pp. 377–389). Newbury Park, CA: Sage.

McCrosky, J. C. (1966). Scales for the measurement of ethos. *Speech Monographs, 33,* 65–72.

McDermott, R. P. (1974). Achieving school failure: An anthropological approach to illiteracy and school failure. In G. D. Spindler (Ed.), *Education and the cultural process* (pp. 82–95). New York: Holt, Rinehart and Winston.

McGregor, D. (1960). *The human side of enterprise.* New York: McGraw-Hill.

Mechanic, D. (1964). Sources of power in lower participants in complex organizations. In W. W. Cooper, H. J. Leavitt, & M. W. Shelley (Eds.), *New perspectives in organizational research* (pp. 136–149). New York: Wiley.

Merriam, S. B. (1988). *Case study research in education: A qualitative approach.* San Francisco: Jossey-Bass.

Merriam-Webster. (1987). *Webster's ninth new collegiate dictionary.* Springfield, MA: Merriam-Webster.

Meyer, J. W., & Rowan, B. (1977). Institutionalized organizations: Formal structure as myth and ceremony. *American Journal of Sociology, 83* (2), 340–363.

Miles, M. B., & Huberman, A. M. (1984). *Qualitative data analysis.* Newbury Park, CA: Sage.

Miles, M. B., & Huberman, A. M. (1994). *Qualitative data analysis: An expanded sourcebook* (2nd ed.). Thousand Oaks, CA: Sage.

Milgram, S. (1974). *Obedience to authority: An experimental view.* New York: Harper & Row.

Mill, J. S. (1979). *Utilitarianism.* Indianapolis, IN: Hackett. (original work published 1861)

Miller, G. R. (1983). Telling it like it isn't and not telling it like it is: Some thoughts on deceptive communication. In J. I. Sisco (Ed.), *The Jensen Lectures: Contemporary communications studies* (pp. 91–116). Tampa: University of South Florida.

Miller, G. R., Mongeau, P. A., & Sleight, C. (1984). *Fudging with friends and lying to lovers: Deceptive communication in interpersonal relationships.* Paper presented at the Second International Conference on Personal Relationships, Madison, WI.

Miller, G. R., Mongeau, P. A., & Sleight, C. (1986). Fudging with friends and lying to lovers: Deceptive communication in interpersonal relationships. *Journal of Social and Personal Relationships, 3*, 495–512.

Miller, G. R., Sleight, C., & deTurck, M. A. (1989). Arousal and attribution: Are the behavioral clues monospecific? In C. V. Roberts & K. W. Watson (Eds.), *Interpersonal communication processes: Original essays* (pp. 273–291). New Orleans: Spectra and Gorsuch Scarisbrick.

Miller, G. R., & Steinberg, M. (1975). *Between people: A new analysis of interpersonal communication.* Chicago: Science Research Associates.

Mintzberg, H. (1983). *Power in and around organizations.* Englewood Cliffs, NJ: Prentice Hall.

Morgan, G. (1986). *Images of organization.* Newbury Park, CA: Sage.

Neuliep, J. W., & Mattson, M. (1990). The use of deception as a compliance-gaining strategy. *Human Communication Research, 16* (3), 409–421.

Norman, R. (1983). *The moral philosophers.* New York: Oxford University Press.

Northouse, P. G. (2001). *Leadership: Theory and practice* (2nd ed.). Thousand Oaks, CA: Sage.

Nyberg, D. (1987). The moral complexity of deception. In D. A. & B. Arnstine (Eds.), *Philosophy of Education, 1987* (pp. 239–252). Normal, IL: Philosophy of Education Society.

Nyberg, D. (1993). *The varnished truth.* Chicago: University of Chicago Press.

Ost, D. H. (1989). The culture of teaching. *The Educational Forum, 53,* (2), 163–118.

O'Toole, J. (1995). *Leading change.* San Francisco: Jossey-Bass.

Palmer, P. (2000). *Let your life speak.* San Francisco: Jossey-Bass.

Parker, W. C. (1985). *Three analyses of stimulated-recall data.* Paper presented at the meeting of the Southwest Educational Research Association, Austin, TX.

Pastin, M. (1986). *The hard choices of management.* San Francisco: Jossey Bass.

Patton, M. Q. (1980). *Qualitative evaluation and research methods.* Beverly Hills, CA: Sage.

Patton, M. Q. (2000). *Qualitative evaluation and research methods* (2nd ed.). Newbury Park, CA: Sage.

Pavlov, I. P. (1927). *Conditioned reflexes.* (G. V. Anrep, Trans.). London: Oxford University Press.

Perrow, C. (1986). *Complex organizations: A critical essay.* New York: Random House.

Plato. (1974). *Plato's Republic.* (G. M. A. Grube, Trans.). Indianapolis, IN: Hackett. (original work 380 BC)

Plato. (1987). *Gorgias.* (D. J. Zeyl, Trans.). Indianapolis: Hackett. (original work 385 BC)

Podair, S. (1965). Language and prejudice toward Negroes. *Phylon, 17,* 390–398.

Pritscher (1987). *Deception, self-direction, and schooling.* Paper presented at the meeting of the Speech Communication Association, Boston.

Putnam, L. L., & Mumby, D. K. (1993). Organizations, emotion and the myth of rationality. In S. Fineman (Ed.), *Emotion in organizations* (pp. 36–57). Newbury Park, CA: Sage.

Radford, J. (1974). Reflections on introspection. *American Psychologist, 4,* 245–250.

Ravitch, D. (2000). *Left back: A century of failed school reforms.* New York: Simon & Schuster.

Rehberg, R. A. & Rosenthal, E. (1978). *Class and merit in the American high school.* New York: Longman.

Revised Code of Washington, RCW § 26.44, § 2, p. 50. (1981).

Revised Code of Washington, RCW § 26.44, § 4, p. 52. (1981).

Revised Code of Washington, RCW § 26.44, § 7, p. 55. (1981).

Revised Code of Washington, RCW § 26.44, § 10, p. 57. (1981).

Riggio, R. E., & Friedman, H. S. (1983). Individual differences and cues to deception. *Journal of Personality and Social Psychology, 45,* 899–915.

Rost, J. C. (1993). *Leadership for the twenty-first century.* Westport, CT: Praeger.

Sarason, S. (1972). Socialization of the leader. In S. Sarason (Ed.), *The creation of settings and future societies* (pp. 181–215). San Francisco: Jossey-Bass.

Sarason, S. (2002). *Educational reform: A self-scrutinizing memoir.* New York: Teachers College Press.

Schaef, A., & Fassel, D. (1988). *The addictive organization.* San Francisco: Harper & Row.

Schein, E. H. (1985). *Organizational culture and leadership.* San Francisco: Jossey-Bass.

Schelling, T. C. (1984). *Choice and consequence.* Cambridge, MA: Harvard University Press.

Schermerhorn, J. R. (1993). *Management for productivity.* New York: Wiley and Sons.

Schwartz, H. S. (1990). *Narcissistic process and corporate decay: The theory of the organization ideal.* New York: New York University Press.

Sears, D. O., Peplau, L. A., & Taylor, S. E. (1991). *Social psychology* (7th ed.). Englewood Cliffs, NJ: Prentice Hall.

Seech, Z. (1988). *Logic in everyday life: Practical reasoning skills.* Belmont, CA: Wadsworth Publishing Company.

Senge, P. M. (1990). *The fifth discipline.* New York: Doubleday/Currency.

Shulman, L. S. (1970). Reconstruction in educational research. *Review of Educational Research, 40,* 371– 396.

Shulman, L. S., & Elstein, A. S. (1975). Studies of problem solving, judgment, and decision making: Implications for educational research. In F. N. Kerlinger (Ed.), *Review of research in education,* Vol. 3. Itasca, IL: Peacock.

Skinner, B. F. (1938). *The behavior of organisms.* New York: Appleton-Century-Crofts.

Skinner, B. F. (1953). *Science and human behavior.* New York: The Free Press.

Skinner, B. F. (1957). The experimental analysis of behavior. *American Scientist, 45,* 343–371.

Skinner, B. F. (1959). *Cumulative record.* New York: Appleton-Century-Crofts.

Skinner, B. F. (1963). Behaviorism at fifty. *Science, 140,* 951–958.

Smircich, L. (1985). Is the concept of culture a paradigm for understanding organizations and ourselves? In P. G. Frost et al. (Eds.), *Organizational culture* (pp. 55–72). Beverly Hills, CA: Sage.

Solomon, R. C. (1992). *Ethics and excellence: Cooperation and integrity in business.* New York: Oxford University Press.

Sorenson, G. (2002). *An intellectual history of leadership studies.* Online publication of the James MacGregor Burns Academy of Leadership, University of Maryland. [http://www.academy.umd.edu/scholarship/casl/articles/sorenson_apsa.htm]

Sowell, T. (1993). *Inside American education.* New York: The Free Press.

Spradley, J. P. (1979). *The ethnographic interview.* New York: Holt, Rinehart and Winston.

Stein, H. F. (1998). *Euphemism, spin, and the crisis in organizational life.* Westport, CT: Quorum Books.

Sterba, J. P. (1991). *Morality in practice* (3rd ed.). Belmont, CA: Wadsworth Publishing Company.

Stiff, J. B., Corman, S. R., & Raghavendra, S. (1991). *Exploring the process of deception detection.* Paper presented at the meeting of the International Communication Association, Chicago.

Stiff, J. B., Kim, H. J., & Ramesh, C. (1992). Truth biases and aroused suspicion in relational deception. *Communication Research, 19,* 326–345.

Stone, D. A. (1988). *Policy, paradox, and political reason.* New York: Harper-Collins.

Stone, K. (1975). The origins of job structures in the steel industry. In R. C. Edwards et al. (Ed.), *Labor market segmentation* (pp. 251–260). Lexington, MA: D. C. Heath.

Sullivan, E. (2001). *The concise book of lying.* New York: Picador USA.

Swenson, R. A. (2004). *Margin: Restoring emotional, physical, financial, and time reserves to overloaded lives.* Colorado Springs, CO: NavPress.

Taylor, F. W. (1911). *Principles of scientific management.* New York: Harper & Row.

Taylor, S. E. (1981). The interface of cognitive and social psychology. In J. Harvey (Ed.), *Cognition and social behavior, and the environment* (pp. 189–212). Hillsdale, NJ: Lawrence Erlbaum.

Thompson, C. M. (2000). *The congruent life: Following the inward path to fulfilling work and inspired leadership.* San Francisco: Jossey-Bass.

Toulmin, S. (1972). *Human understanding: The collective use and evolution of concepts.* Princeton, NJ: Princeton University Press.

Tuckman, B. W. (1965). Developmental sequence in small groups. *Psychological Bulletin, 63,* 384–399.

Turner, R. E., Edgely, C., & Olmstead, G. (1975). Information control in conversation: Honesty is not always the best policy. *Kansas Journal of Sociology, 11,* 69–89.

Twain, M. (1923). *On the damned human race.* New York: Hill & Wang.

Tyler, T. R., & Devintz, V. (1981). Self-serving bias in the attribution of responsibility: Cognitive versus motivational explanations. *Journal of Experimental Social Psychology, 17,* 408–416.

Van Manen, M. (1990). *Researching lived experience.* London, Ontario: State University of New York Press.

Watson, J. B. (1919). *Psychology from the standpoint of a behaviorist.* Philadelphia: Lippincott.

Weber, M. (1947). *The theory of social and economic organization* (T. Parsons, Trans.). New York: Free Press. (original work published 1927)

Weick, K. E. (1976, March). Educational organizations as loosely coupled systems. *Administrative Science Quarterly, 21*, 1–19.

Weick, K. E. (1995). *Sensemaking in organizations*. Thousand Oaks, CA: Sage.

Weiner, B. (1979). A theory of motivation for some classroom experiences. *Journal of Educational Psychology, 71*, 3–25.

Weiner, B. (1980). A cognitive (attribution)-emotion-action model of motivated behavior: An analysis of judgments of help-giving. *Journal of Personality and Social Psychology, 39*, 186–200.

Weiner, B. (1986). *An attributional theory of motivation and emotion*. New York: Springer Verlag.

Weston, A. (2000). *A rulebook for arguments* (3rd ed.). Indianapolis, IN: Hackett.

Whaley, B. (1982). Toward a general theory of deception. *Journal of Strategic Studies, 5*, 185, 192.

Wicklund, R. A., & Frey, D. (1980). Self-awareness theory: When the self makes a difference. In D. M. Wegner & R. R. Vallacher (Eds.), *The self in social psychology* (pp. 31–54). New York: Oxford University Press.

Wright, R. (1936). *Uncle Tom's children*. New York: Harper & Row.

X, M. (1964). *The autobiography of Malcolm X*. New York: Grove Press.

Yinger, R. J. (1986). *Examining thought in action: A theoretical and methodological critique of research on interactive teaching*. Paper presented at the annual meeting of the American Educational Research Association, San Francisco.

Zubay, B., & Soltis, J. F. (2005). *Creating the ethical school*. New York: Teachers College Press.

Index

About the Author

Dan Mahoney, born in the beautiful state of Montana, is a lifelong educator. He earned his B.A. at The Evergreen State College in Olympia, Washington, and began teaching in 1978. After teaching in all grade levels in public and private schools, and in a residential treatment setting, he earned his Ph.D. at Gonzaga University where he now teaches courses in ethics, educational evaluation, and curricular design in the Department of Educational Leadership and Administration. He and his wife, Scooter, live in Spokane, Washington.